Dance of Disruption and Creation

'It is a book that both senior leaders and business school students will find useful and practical.'
Professor Costas Markides, *London Business School*

'I recommend this book to anyone who is a student of strategy and successful business.'
Peter Brabeck-Letmathe, *Chairman Emeritus of Nestlé S.A.*

It's an exciting time to be alive! We are witness to an epoch of change, a dance of disruption and creation, that is re-imagining our world. Where are these disruptions coming from? What opportunities do they uncover? How can one make sense of them? And most importantly, how should one prepare and act? This book, written by two influential business leaders, unpacks these "epochal" changes and how they represent a defining moment of opportunity for the world of business.

Nandu Nandkishore and Neeraj Chandra draw upon diverse sources, academic literature, discussions with CEOs, startup founders and experts, in order to understand the significant pivots of change emerging from a wide canvas and then stitch together a perspective of an exciting, brave new world. Unlike many other books that focus only on emerging technologies, the authors here look at disruption through several lenses: technology, demographics, economic change, the changing nature of institutions, and the interplay of technology as it fundamentally shapes consumers and society. The book goes beyond describing changes taking place. It explores the "why so" and "so what" to provide an understanding of the shifts taking place, and crucially, the implications for the world of enterprise. Using simple examples and frameworks throughout, the book provides specific, action-oriented solutions that businesses can employ.

This book will be of specific interest to business leaders, strategists, investment professionals, as well as social scientists and public servants. It is for change-makers who are excited to seize the unique opportunity that this change represents – to build competitive advantage, re-invent markets and enterprise, and indeed, to make the world a better place.

A selection of reference links and material for the book is accessible at www.routledge.com/ 9781032184791.

Nandu Nandkishore and **Neeraj Chandra** are friends and batch-mates from IIM Ahmedabad, each with 40 years of experience working in global multinationals like Nestlé and Unilever in senior leadership roles, being on company boards, mentoring startups, and teaching at business school. They bring to this book their deep reflections and insights from years of accumulated global experience, from their vast network of experts, and curated from their extensive readings.

Dance of Disruption and Creation

Dear Marco,

Keep challenging thinking.

Epochal Change and the Opportunity for Enterprise

& growing !!

NANDU NANDKISHORE AND NEERAJ CHANDRA

Warmly,

Nandu

Routledge
Taylor & Francis Group

LONDON AND NEW YORK

Cover design and illustrations: Elephant | India

First published 2024
by Routledge
4 Park Square, Milton Park, Abingdon, Oxon OX14 4RN

and by Routledge
605 Third Avenue, New York, NY 10158

Routledge is an imprint of the Taylor & Francis Group, an informa business

© 2024 Nandu Nandkishore and Neeraj Chandra

The right of Nandu Nandkishore and Neeraj Chandra to be identified as authors of this work has been asserted in accordance with sections 77 and 78 of the Copyright, Designs and Patents Act 1988.

British Library Cataloguing-in-Publication Data
A catalogue record for this book is available from the British Library

Library of Congress Cataloging-in-Publication Data
Names: Nandkishore, Nandu, author. | Chandra, Neeraj, author.
Title: Dance of disruption and creation : epochal change and the
   opportunity for enterprise / Nandu Nandkishore and Neeraj Chandra.
Description: Abingdon, Oxon ; New York, NY : Routledge, 2024. |
   Includes bibliographical references and index. |
Identifiers: LCCN 2023007632 (print) | LCCN 2023007633 (ebook) |
   ISBN 9781032184784 (hardback) | ISBN 9781032184791 (paperback) |
   ISBN 9781003254737 (ebook)
Subjects: LCSH: Organizational change. | Disruptive technologies.
Classification: LCC HD58.8 .N359 2024 (print) | LCC HD58.8 (ebook) |
   DDC 658.406—dc23/eng/20230303
LC record available at https://lccn.loc.gov/2023007632
LC ebook record available at https://lccn.loc.gov/2023007633

ISBN: 978-1-032-18478-4 (hbk)
ISBN: 978-1-032-18479-1 (pbk)
ISBN: 978-1-003-25473-7 (ebk)

DOI: 10.4324/9781003254737

Typeset in Minion
by Apex CoVantage, LLC

Access the Support Material: www.routledge.com/9781032184791

Contents

Foreword

I have known Nandu since the time I became global CEO of Nestlé and he was a young and promising manager at Nestlé. He had already built a reputation for being a great marketer and effective leader across cultures. In the years since, I sponsored his career growth and watched with pride as he grew in his leadership skills and communication to become one of our top global talents.

After retirement from Nestlé, he has become a venture capitalist, an academic who teaches at London Business School and the Indian School of Business, and is also on a few company boards. One thing hasn't changed over the years: he thinks deeply about all that is happening around us and what this means for business.

I am glad to see him come together with his friend Neeraj (who has an illustrious career with Unilever India) to pen a book on disruption and what lessons enterprise could learn to deal with disruption more effectively. I have contributed a small story to this book, which he has added into the last section on strategy recommendations.

How to deal with disruption – and create companies that sustainably create value for a long time – is a key question that CEO and others would do well to ponder. This is a question on which I myself have spoken often and at various forums. I am glad to note that Nandu has been following my thoughts closely!

I recommend this book to anyone who is a student of strategy and successful business. It is told from the point of view of a practitioner and a global manager. I wish you enjoyable reading!!

Peter Brabeck-Letmathe,
Chairman Emeritus, Nestle S.A., Former Chairman
and CEO of Nestle S.A., Former Chairman
of Formula One

Foreword

Over the past 20 years, academic researchers have been exploring the question: "How can companies respond to disruption successfully?" As a result, we have now developed a rich understanding of what differentiates success from failure in responding to disruption. One of the most important things we have learned is that it is a mistake to approach disruption as a threat; and it is equally a mistake to approach it as an opportunity. It is best to start one's thinking by looking at disruption as both a threat and an opportunity. This has serious implications in that it requires companies to develop strategies that can simultaneously defend against the threat and attack the opportunity.

This raises the question: "What sort of strategy would allow a company to defend and attack at the same time?" The answer is: "An innovative strategy!" An effective strategy of response must avoid imitating what others have done in response to the disruption and should instead help the firm differentiate itself as much as possible. Simply trying to be better than the disruptors themselves or the other industry rivals responding to the same disruption is not enough. In this sense, the firm is not looking for a strategy of response – it is looking for a strategy that would allow it to reposition and differentiate itself by taking advantage of disruption.

While the idea is simple enough – just develop an innovative strategy of response – the reality is that established firms face formidable obstacles in following such advice. Creativity is in short supply in organisations, and the evidence is that big companies are not very good at escaping their own mental models and corporate orthodoxies. This is exactly where this book by Nandu and Neeraj will come handy. Based on the cumulative wisdom of two seasoned and successful business executives, the book provides insights, "aha" moments, and common-sense suggestions that will get the creative juices of the reader flowing. The authors do not pretend to have answers but offer, instead, numerous counterintuitive ways for companies to think creatively about the challenge of responding to the disruptions facing them. It is a book that both senior leaders as well as business school students will find useful and practical. It deserves to be on the shelf of any manager facing the challenge of disruption.

Professor Costas Markides,
London Business School

Preface

We live in a world of epochal change.

As we saw first-hand, big, powerful streams of change coalesce around us, we felt compelled to write this book, to record and summarise the key changes, to help to make sense of it, and also to understand the implications for markets . . . for our world, for enterprise, investors, social scientists, and public servants. Or just curious thinkers.

We have tried to paint, in broad brush strokes, the big changes underway. And to suggest how this could translate into action for us. As individuals. As enterprise leaders. Or as change makers.

This book, while based on our experience, reflections, and observations, draws also upon diverse sources, academic literature, discussions with CEOs, startup founders, and experts in other fields to identify the significant pivots of change emerging from a wide canvas – and then stitch together a perspective of an exciting, brave new world that is being born.

We hope these perspectives trigger opportunities for enterprise, for further study in academia, and for change makers to create even more magic.

We feel privileged to be living through and witnessing first-hand this tsunami of change. We hope you read this book with the same sense of wonder that we wrote it with. And with a sense of excitement at the unique opportunity to create a difference and leave the world a better place.

Acknowledgements

It is not easy, with a work that tries to document this tsunami of change, to acknowledge all the people who, knowingly or otherwise, helped shape our journey. Certainly, we owe a big vote of thanks to the various authors and thinkers who we refer to in the various endnotes or in the References section.

We also owe a sincere thank you to Professor Costas Markides, of London Business School, and to Peter Brabeck, Chairman Emeritus of Nestle SA, who challenged us and helped us refine and shape our rough thoughts into their current form. They have both generously contributed forewords to this book.

We owe thanks also to our editor, Bruce Wexler, who unerringly (and with kindness) pointed out our various inconsistencies and repetitions. And our design house in India, "Elephant", led by Ashwini and Sanjana, who helped hammer the book into its current shape.

We thank also our colleagues and extended network of friends and connections, too numerous to list individually, who acted as sounding boards and helped sharpen our thoughts on various facets. We owe a lot to the various people and experiences we have had along our careers who helped shape our responses to this maelstrom of change and figure out what works.

A big and special thank you to our spouses, Indu and Shalini, who supported us on this difficult journey over the last year. By helping us make time, listen to our doubts and theories, helping us make sense, and by helping proofread and correct the flow. And to our families, children (and grandchildren!) for patiently encouraging and having faith in us. And giving us time!!

Finally, and most importantly, we thank you, dear reader, for being a part of our journey. We hope you not only enjoy the book but will partner with us via our website in helping shape the future evolution of this book. We dedicate this book to you.

Chapter 1. Introduction

Epochal Change and Enterprise

The Opportunity in Disruption

Today, we live in a world of dramatic and disruptive change. This epochal dance of disruption and creation, this tsunami of change is radically transforming and unleashing a new world of possibilities.

What is this change, what does it mean and what can we do about it?

This book is for those who believe in the opportunity this change represents. It is about sensing the sources of the change, right from those societal changes happening under our noses, to the blur of technology driven shifts. It is about understanding this change and seeking out opportunities in it.

It is also about the imperative for action to seize these opportunities.

A WORLD OF CHANGE, A CHANGE OF OUR WORLD

We see **seismic shifts in society underway** – changes that are fundamentally altering every facet of our lives. "Suddenly" we seem to be different. Different in the way we transact, we educate; in our relationships, the way we socialise, our geo-politics, what we consume, and even what we think!

Some shifts are led by technology. Others arise out of underlying changes in human societies and institutions.

New technologies are transforming the world of possibilities at a dizzying pace. Some, like drones, extend the reach of our actions to new dimensions!

As we well know, the last 50,000 years of human history, have periodically seen **epochal changes which have driven and shaped our civilisation.**

The shift to agriculture from earlier hunter gatherer societies was a pivotal change that enabled early civilisation. Related shifts like the domestication of animals and the invention of the wheel revolutionised and helped the creation of kingdoms and empires.

Changes that fundamentally altered the way we lived and our identities.

The industrial revolution starting in the 19th century was yet another epochal change dramatically increasing productivity, spreading widespread prosperity and changing life fundamentally across the world.

New dimensions have even been added to our existence. Digital identities exist in a parallel, digital universe. And this changes our very concept of self-identity, family, and society.

DOI: 10.4324/9781003254737-1

Life as we humans knew it is changing fundamentally, once again (see box) and on a scale like never before.

THE CHANGE IS SUPER-FAST, with the first 20 years of this century driving disruptive developments with greater impact than the 150 years prior. Today, we cannot imagine life without the internet, smart phones, Google, and social media. Yet none of these existed in everyday life barely 20 years go. Change that took a millennium to impact during the agrarian transition took a century with the advent of the industrial age and is today showing up within a decade. Or even sooner.

THE CHANGE IS HUGE: Over a third of our world (in Asia) has tripled its income over the last two decades . . . More than it did in the century prior! Within five years, digital finance in China has grown from a million users to over 200 million.

According to an article in the Economist, mobile financial transactions have transformed life and business in Kenya, with up to 25% of GDP now being transacted digitally.

THE CHANGE IS UBIQUITOUS: Silicon Valley has been at the forefront of change, and it is to be expected that life today is different in the Bay area. But life has altered even more so for Shu Chi from Shanghai, Manuel from Manila, or even Balu from Bangalore, and in almost every way!

Disruptive change: a change that can only be called **"epochal"**.

I. Disruption – the dance of destruction and creation, and the role of enterprise

Today, enterprise is at the epicentre of change.

The central role of enterprise and trade in our lives emerged with the agricultural revolution. As hunter gatherers transitioned to an agrarian society the concept of barter and trade took shape. Markets started to determine the prosperity of a changing society. Sinews of trade like the silk route, the exchanges around the pool of the Mediterranean, helped the evolution of nation states.

Post the industrial revolution, a new world and a new phase of enterprise can be seen.
Manufacturing in the industrial era fuelled the growth, concentration and development of a much wider world of enterprise. New models of enterprise and new industrial scale products emerged to take advantage of the engines of the industrial revolution-power & mechanisation of production. The world of enterprise found new roots - delivering life needs but with immensely more output. And going further to open up new possibilities and frontiers e.g. the railways and electricity. The changing world of **enterprise now had a new centrality** in shaping our lives.

It is the energy for the change. Our lives revolve around the products and services we use. As enterprise and its products transform, the lives we live transform.

And enterprise gets driven to reinvent itself by disruptive shifts in technology and societal needs. A change that is a foundation for great, new opportunities also sees the withering away of an old order.

Today, the scale and extent of disruption has meant that over half of the Fortune 500 companies from 30 years ago don't exist anymore. In the 1920s, the estimated life of a "Fortune 500" company (the term probably wasn't used then but refers to the largest companies) was about 90 years. Fast forward half a century and this had dropped to 60 years. Today, the expected life is closer to 15 years. Many stalwarts of yesteryear have completely disappeared. General Electric, which was a mainstay of the Fortune 500, announced a split into three entities which may well be taken off that list. One look at the world's top 10 corporations today, and we find names like Apple, Amazon, Alphabet, Facebook, Microsoft, Netflix, some of which did not even exist 20 years ago!

Morphing markets. The tumult of technology. And more.

Nobody is immune. Witness the story of Kodak – a company that pioneered photography and dominated the 20th century with the omnipresent "Kodak Moment". They invented digital photography and worked with it for two decades before realising there was no money to be made through digital photography. They closed down their digital photography division in 1998 to focus on their comfort zone: paper-based photography. Ten years later, the company had closed down.

Even as the need and ability to capture moments into images was democratised by technology to become ubiquitous, photography had migrated to phones!

Apple is another great example. The launch of their first "smart phone" – iPhone – cannibalised and destroyed the iPod. And destroyed Nokia at the same time. Ironically, this happened with the launch of the smart phone, something that Nokia had developed and launched earlier. But they couldn't or didn't imagine the potential of what they could have done with the smart phone which brought together a digital camera, a phone, and a small computer into one compact device. Apple did imagine. Samsung and others followed. The rest is history.

Ironically, Nokia themselves were disruptors in 1998 when they toppled global market leader Motorola with the launch of digital-technology-enabled mobile phones. Nokia quickly went global and dominated markets around the world. But only for under a decade. It appears incumbency doesn't count for much in today's disruptive world. If anything, the hubris of success and a proven business model can blind one to new possibilities. This is a sobering lesson for the speed with which models can be disrupted.

Not only are the needs addressed by enterprise changing – the way enterprises create consumer and financial value is also changing.

New technologies are emerging, transforming the world of possibilities at a dizzying pace.

Markets are morphing and business models are changing. Cameras have vanished, but photographs have multiplied. The biggest retailer has no stores. The largest taxi company today owns no taxis. The largest hotel chain owns no hotels.

The composition of the world enterprise is changing. Welcome to a brave new world of start-ups, prodigy corporations, and re-invented companies. They are harvesting the opportunity, building scale, and setting the agenda like never before. A quarter of total market capitalisation value in the US stock market is now in IT companies, most of which have started in this century. Prodigy corporations like Alibaba have grown and today shaped billions in business value and changed the life of billions. The start-up eco-system reflects the immense possibilities of change, and mythology is being made by unicorns of a different kind.

The world of disruption is also a world of unprecedented creation and opportunity.

2. Implications

The scale and extent of this disruption can be **a scary challenge** for marketers and business people.

The success of large, stable businesses is a disincentive for rapid change. But, as Gary Hamel wrote in his book "What matters now", "Somewhere out there is a bullet with your company's name on it. You're just going to have to shoot first". In other words, if you don't disrupt your own business model, someone out there will do it to you. This is a big change from the "if it ain't broken, don't fix it mind-set" that characterised most of last century.

Many powerful disruptions are changing our world. They are reimagining our world and the structure of our industry. Disruptions could come from anywhere. Who would have imagined in 1990 that the cellular phone industry would be the death knell of the photographic film industry by the turn of the century. Which disruption do we watch out for?

Ideally, we would like our company to be the disruptor that makes other enterprises the dinosaurs. But embracing a new disruptive opportunity is also fraught with risk. Because one doesn't know if the opportunity is indeed worth pursuing, or whether it will turn out to be significant. In the process, it is easy to take one's eye off the ball, allowing existing businesses to slide. For instance, Kodak chased the digital photography opportunity for two decades only to give it up as commercially unviable.

There are large, new opportunities arising in this epoch of change. Some arise out of underlying changes in demographics or urbanisation or economics.

New needs felt by these emerging segments, new technologies, and new ways of delivering advantage are all creating opportunities that dwarf even the largest of today's businesses.

The canvas of this change is pervasive. From an era where disruption was restricted to "technology" industries, the poster children of transformation today are in everyday domains – taxis, hotels, and retailing. Disruption is extending from the business of technology to technology in business – every business! It is reaching out to every domain and scale of present and possible enterprise. Change presents an opportunity, not just in the products and markets addressed by business, but also the way business is conducted. In every process, every function. Business models are being reinvented even as we write this.

How does one identify the disruption that is headed one's way? And once we identify it, what are the challenges and how can one prepare for it?

Is there an opportunity one can seize? Can one address new and different markets? Or address a market differently?

How does this affect underlying consumer behaviours? We look at these and other questions in this book.

Whether a challenge or an opportunity, addressing a new need or adopting a business model, for a large or for a small business, epochal change makes it imperative to act. If we have not leveraged change in whatever we do, we probably are missing out on an opportunity of a lifetime. **Today, change is the opportunity.**

This book is about the understanding the change and acting on it.

3. See the change

- We live in a world where we already start to feel an acceleration of change. The dominant sense is of a change in technology: a series of probably fuzzily understood, technological disruptions – largely digital.

- But we also see fundamental shifts in "who we are" and "what we think". Changes which are having as powerful an impact.

  For the first time in world history, the majority of world citizenry is urban. And demographic pyramids are getting inverted. Instead of "a lot of young people and a few ageing seniors", the proportions are starting to reverse.

  We are living through this change. Let's try to understand the magnitude and the subtleties of the social shifts underway. By the turn of this decade, a third of our world (India/China) – almost 3 billion people – could have had almost a tenfold growth in their income since the year 2000. Imagine the impact on the lives and societies of 3 billion people when they earn ten times what they did a few decades earlier.

- Disruptive knowledge and technology are powerful forces but, as they ripple through human lives, their impact multiplies many fold. For instance, it is the widespread adoption of social media – and not merely the tech behind it – that has transformed our lives.

Rather than just glimpse this maelstrom of tech-driven change as a blur, we seek to understand the fundamental impact of these technologies upon our lives and the possibilities that arise.

- Even as we identify the key pivots of this change, we believe a **"WHY SO" AND "SO WHAT"** approach is vital to use, in order to understand the opportunity and seize it.

4. Do the change

A few key questions to ask of ourselves to live up to our **"Action Mantra"**:

DOES OUR ENTERPRISE BELIEVE that change is an opportunity? Or are we largely maintaining a continuity with a not so distant (but disrupted) past?

HOW CAN WE BUILD THE CONFIDENCE AND CLARITY TO ACT? We need to start seeing the changes with perspective, with insight and foresight on how the world is being reshaped; recognise the profundity of the change and the opportunities being thrown up. This is a precursor to Action.

DO WE HAVE THE NECESSARY TOOL KIT TO DRIVE ACTION? For example, how do we address the dilemma of continuity versus change? The tension between Value creation and Value capture?

5. About this book

In the first two sections of the book, we will identify some of the key seismic changes that are unfolding. We will look at changes coming out of:

- Demographics

- Rapidly evolving consumer attitudes

- The evolving economic environment

- Morphing institutions

- The digital and tech disruption in its myriad avatars

- Technology and business models

Is there a difference in how a large company should respond versus how a startup should respond? Can a large company reinvent itself to be a value creator? How?

What is the approach that will help us seize the opportunity?

We look at these questions in the third section of this book.

Our focus in the last third of the book is on **how to act** on these disruptions and seize the opportunity. We examine the challenges involved, identify the key tools, and suggest ways to successfully seize the Opportunity.

The book emphasises the pervasiveness of the change and its impact on virtually every facet of business, in all industries and across geographies. However, it does have **a bias towards consumer** markets. We believe the ultimate market for all goods and services and industrial activity is the consumer market. And therefore, changes in the consumer market will, in fact, cascade through the value chain of all industries.

The opportunity of change is rippling through the world, and our illustrations reflect this diversity. We are also bringing into focus the shifts in geographies like China, India, and Africa, which are not only large population centres but which are also leapfrogging generations of technological change and seeing tectonic shifts.

6. An invitation to explore and collaborate

The canvas of this change opportunity is **enormous** and by no stretch of imagination can we, as authors, even begin to capture it fully. We have attempted to share perspectives on the change, as also frameworks which can help one engage with, and act on it. But we do seek your involvement and inputs to make this a living document that will continue to guide us in this journey.

Part I

Who We Are
The Transformation of Society

We live in an era of dramatic change. And sense a blur of technological shifts.

Knowledge and technology are, indeed, powerful forces transforming our world. Not so apparent, but equally disruptive, is how we as people and as a society have transformed.

FOR THE FIRST TIME EVER IN HUMAN HISTORY. . .

- Our demographic pyramid is now inverted! We have more people over the age of 65, compared to children under five.

- Every second human is urban. From a largely rural, agrarian species, we have become (sophisticated?) town dwellers.

- A third of the world has tripled its income since the turn of 21st century – more affluence created than in the previous 500 years.

Fundamental changes are taking place in who we are and what we think. At a pace like never before and on a scale like never before.

How is this transforming consumer behaviour, and in turn the markets, opportunities, enterprise models, and innovation built around them?

In this section, we look at these socio-economic changes. In us as individuals. In our collective institutions. In society. And in the implications for the world of enterprise.

DOI: 10.4324/9781003254737-2

Chapter 2
Economic Transformation
The Surge in Emerging Markets

Seismic economic shifts are under way. We are used to a global reality where the Western economies accounted for the bulk of value creation and consumption. However, the surging economic "South" already accounts for 50% of global GDP and the bulk of growth. How does this impact our world? What does this mean for business, innovation, and investments?

Economic growth and development are intensely studied subjects, matters of paramount interest for economists, administrators, and businesses alike. Our focus, however, is not to delve into the root cause of economic growth nor to discuss how to enhance it.

Instead, we examine the economic shifts happening in our world today, recognise their centrality, and highlight their unprecedented scale. And we emphasise their game-changing impact on our world – in particular, that of enterprise.

We look at:

1. **The surge in the emerging markets: the economic "South"**

2. **The impact of economic growth**

3. **The economic South: a new engine for the world economy**

4. **Economic growth and the forces of change**

I. ECONOMIC TRANSFORMATION – THE SURGE IN THE SOUTH

The world is today going through an economic transformation like never before. What is transforming the world today is **the surge of the economic "South"**, which is seeing significantly faster growth, at scale, with an impact that is disruptive and not merely incremental. A few facts:

- **INCOMES HAVE SURGED**. Incomes in India and China have tripled in the previous century and could triple again by 2030. Compare this with the average of 2% p.a. economic growth recorded in the 19th century and the 2% per century in the centuries prior.

DOI: 10.4324/9781003254737-3

Economic growth in key cities like Delhi and Shanghai is even higher, with average nominal incomes being ten times that at the turn of the century.

- **THE BREADTH OF THIS CHANGE IS MASSIVE.** Almost 2 billion people have been lifted above the poverty line in the economic "South" over the last two decades. And this shift is showing no sign of slowing. Potentially, over 5 billion people are moving from poverty towards prosperity, and at unprecedented speed.

The Asian transformation is spreading across the continent. Countries like Bangladesh, once associated with poverty and suffering, have become frontrunners in economic progress. Latin America is stepping up and Africa is emerging as the next big economic opportunity.

How does this change lives and what are the opportunities for enterprise? How does the structure of the world and its economy change with this discontinuous income growth that affects **two thirds** of its population?

2. BEYOND THE STATISTICS, A PHENOMENAL LIFE IMPACT

"Development is about transforming the lives of people, not just transforming economies" – Joseph Stiglitz.

Economic growth, at any time, has had a strong link with human progress and quality of life. Often facilitated by conditions like stability of governance and benign natural forces, it has been one of the primary engines of human prosperity and quality of life.

A) Economic growth is a powerful instrument that helps alleviate poverty

If we are to meet the UN sustainable development goals (SDG), sustainable Economic Growth is critical in order to reduce or eliminate poverty – particularly extreme poverty, with people living on under $1 per day.

Research that compares the experiences of a wide range of developing countries supports the hypothesis that sustained and rapid economic growth is the most important lever to raise populations out of poverty. Having grown up as the first generation in a newly independent, poor and socialist India, the authors can personally vouch for the power in this argument.

"Historically nothing has worked better than economic growth in enabling societies to improve the life chances of their members, including those at the very bottom", observes Dani Rodrik, in his paper at Harvard University.

B) A transformation in quality of life

Economic growth goes hand in hand with education and better access to health and services. And with it comes a far superior quality of life: longer life, healthier life, and hopefully, a more fulfilling life. Economic growth is perhaps the single biggest engine in this transformation of life, even as factors like income distribution and development of HDI are equally central to progress.

In his path breaking treatise "Development is Freedom", Nobel laureate Amartya Sen has described economic growth "as a crucial means for expanding substantive freedoms. . . . These freedoms are strongly associated with improvements in general living standards, such as greater opportunities for people to become healthier, eat better and live longer".

And so, not only does growth drive human development; human development, in turn, feeds economic growth in a virtuous cycle, as people get more skilled and free to participate in shaping and simultaneously benefiting from economic growth.

C) An accelerated change in consumption, markets, and lifestyles

Growth and development are often summarised in monetary terms, most commonly expressed as "per capita income". However, this abstraction does not reflect the enormity of the change that is happening:

• For the common man, economic growth, beyond the mathematical abstraction, is about the access to goods and services that enable a better quality of life. And a lot is changing as growth accelerates and income doubles or triples for Maria from Manila or Manav from Mumbai. In a relatively short span of a decade, patterns are changing: consumption of existing categories is increasing and new categories are making an entry. Consumption of personal care categories and processed food has increased. Leisure and lifestyle products have made an entry. And new spaces like consumer finance are taking root.

  Consumer goods companies have historically invested in market creation, with great success. New competitors who have been faster off the block have created higher value categories in the market and greater economic weight for themselves. And, as economies move up the income curve, markets are seeing accelerated growth and opportunities across a broader spectrum of new consumer-facing categories.

• In parallel, large parts of the labour pool are shifting away from agriculture; industry and services are becoming the new growth opportunity. More capital is getting employed in economic activities, and this shift to capital in itself generates a new economy. Geographically the large urban pockets are becoming the hub of the country, affecting not just the economy but also the body politic of the country.

• There is an upstream surge in infrastructure and social assets. The recent commissioning of the Padma Bridge in Bangladesh illustrates the opportunity – and virtuous cycle – of investments in infrastructure. Built at a cost of $3.9 billion, a symbol of Bangladesh's economic development, it is expected to significantly cut road and rail transits for over 25% of the country's population. And enhance GDP growth between 1.3–2.0% per annum!

Large opportunities are opening up in services and capital goods, accompanied by a transformation of investments, entrepreneurship, and governance. Indeed, this reinforces our belief that the consumer market is the ultimate market that drives all economic activity.

3. THE WORLD ECONOMY HAS A NEW ENGINE

The surge in the South is enabling 5 billion people to enter the world economy. Not merely consuming off its fringes but actually actively participating in it and contributing to its enduring growth.

A) New entrants to the world economy: seizing the surge opportunity

In 1996, Prof CK Prahlad first highlighted the opportunity at the bottom of the pyramid where demand could be tapped, despite low incomes. Today, this economic base is becoming much larger. And is often the source of innovation that migrates across the entire market and even becomes the foundation for new opportunities in the developed world.

The opportunity here is not merely that of extending trickle-down historical solutions to an emerging market of 5 billion. The needs of this group are different, often arising out of the juxtaposition of a mind-set of frugality with a heightened desire for consumption.

The industry opportunity is to find **new solutions** which bridge the frugality/consumption paradox. In developing markets, sachets and low-unit packs have built large consumption markets. More recently, prepaid subscriptions have driven growth in the telecom markets.

With continued economic growth, emerging technologies are creating new opportunities to "leapfrog" conventional market development stages with innovative value-added services. A good example is the way developing economies have skipped fixed-line telephony and jumped straight to mobile phones.

Or in the manner in which digital banking is creating access for people who have never seen the inside of a conventional bank. It showcases how technological innovation can break the fundamental barriers of accessibility and affordability to unlock these vast markets. Also the opportunity for governments to build financial inclusion and further reinforce growth.

B) Sustained high growth of emerging economies

The world is today at an inflexion point where emerging economies, led by China and other Asian countries, are showing strong economic growth, even as growth in the Western world slows down. The world now has a new economic engine in the traditional "South": a consuming class that actively participates in and shapes the global economy. Emerging markets today are breaching the inflexion point for sustained growth (see box).

Their large population weight and the demographics of young educated workers dramatically increases the power of this surge. With each passing year, the future direction of the global economy depends more on growth in the "South".

As accelerated change happens, the relative importance of markets changes rapidly. Today, China is the largest market for Apple phones. Even in the relatively mature automobiles category, China accounts for almost 30% of the world market.

The Chinese economy has seen multifaceted development (see graphic). Would emerging markets potentially see similar growth?

TRANSFORMED ECONOMIC STRUCTURE

"The transition from a zero-sum to a positive-sum economy is the most important change in economic history" *...... our world in data.org.

Historically, as long as land was the primary factor of economic production, growth remained slow and wealth accumulation was a zero sum game. The only way to become richer was to acquire others' lands and for 'them' to become poorer.

This is no longer the case.

The most important impact of the industrial revolution has been the possibility that people invest talent and capital to create wealth, whereby everybody benefits! Economic Growth and human development can thereby generate a virtuous circle of prosperity and opportunity.

We may think of China as a special case, but large markets like India are also starting to grow. Today, the Indian market for mobile phones is probably the

10 TECHNOLOGY LEADERSHIP
Contender for world leadership in several areas eg 5G, AI, Supercomputing.

01 GDP GROWTH
(since economic reform-1978)
~ 8-10% per year

09 TECH-BASED NEW BUSINESSES
Local companies lead domestic markets. A strengthening global footprint, challenging world leaders. A significant and growing engine for its economy. High turnover and valuations.

02 POVERTY UPLIFTMENT
800 million people

08 MANUFACTURING
Base for the world, across categories.

03 HDI
A significant improvement (access to health, education, and other services)

CHINA
A leading indicator for the surge in the south?

07 OTHER SERVICES
Amongst global leaders in transportation, real estate, banking and construction.

04 CONSUMER GOODS
From being a country of rationing to a consumer driven economy. The largest market for luxury goods.

06 NEW MARKETS TRAVEL & TOURISM
~$1 Trillion to GDP.

05 RETAIL
Has the world's largest shopping centers. Wholesaling & retail contributed ~$2 trillion to GDP.

largest in the world. The user base of Facebook is almost 300 million – amongst the largest in the world. The Indian subsidiary for Unilever commands a valuation close to that of its parent company.

Other countries, albeit smaller (though in many cases they have populations significantly larger than most developed countries), are also starting to grow fast.

Imagine a scenario from the future where economies like Bangladesh, Indonesia, or Vietnam become as large as the German economy! This hypothetical reality may well be possible in the future. Indeed, we have seen examples of transformation like South Korea, where its sizeable economic shifts would not have been imaginable a few decades earlier.

The global pool of active consumers is now triple the base of barely a few decades earlier. Scanning and seizing opportunities with this new pool is perhaps one of the biggest opportunities today.

C) Shifting economic pendulums

Economic and power pendulums have shifted more than once over the last 2,000 years.

Starting with the Industrial Revolution and the advent of colonisation enabled by "Guns, Germs, and Steel"* (ref. the book of this name by Jared Diamond), the global economic pendulum shifted decisively to the North Atlantic economies of Europe and America – so much so that they dominated global trade throughout the 19th and 20th centuries.

Over the last 300 years, the developed countries have led the world – be it economic growth, scientific innovation, or even crusading for human rights or international causes. Today, however, we see economic pendulums and the **"global centre of Economic gravity"** swinging decisively back towards East, where it had resided for millennia before the 1800s.[1]

China and India (the former more definitively than the latter) have re-entered the list of leading world economies. At the time of writing, China is #2 in global aggregate GDP and India is at #5. (These are in US dollar measures. In PPP terms, they would be larger.)

The surge in the south and an increased "flattening" of the world is leading to new economic poles (China) and a shift to a new, multi-polar world. Witness the ambitious initiative of China's One Belt, One Road that seeks to transform – and dominate – how the world moves goods across continents, through a system of roads and maritime links.

This trend began in the last 20 years of the 20th century, with the East Asian economic miracle spreading from Japan to Korea and the ASEAN tigers, and was accelerated by China's liberalisation in 1980, with India following suit in 1991.

The emerging markets' immediate business opportunities are in East Asia, with the birth of the "ASEAN +6" concept – which includes China, Japan, South Korea, Australia, New Zealand, and possibly India (though that last is still open to question) – as quite possibly the largest economic zone ever seen in history, with over 3 billion human beings in it.

In a similar fashion, Africa is home to the next big trend that will emerge. From "one in every 25" humans on the planet being African in the year 1900, by the end of this century, "one in every four" humans will be African because of improved healthcare, nutrition, and governance. With a population well in excess of a billion, Africa would have a working-age population exceeding that of India. This implies that we might well see in this century, in Africa, a mirror of the "Asian economic boom" we saw over the last 50 years.

Playing in these economic zones and managing the cross-border trade of goods and services will create huge opportunities. Governments and corporations can ill afford to ignore these emerging powerhouses.

4. THE NEXUS: ECONOMICS, TECHNOLOGY, AND DISRUPTIVE TRANSFORMATIONS

Economic growth and the forces of change

Historically, the most disruptive transformations in human life have been related to profound changes in the nature of the economy and its productivity.

The transition from hunter-gatherer to settled agriculture (the Neolithic Revolution) was the first big shift. The **disruptive "technology"** of agriculture in a nomadic world transformed the economic foundation of mankind. It impacted the size of output and the economy, providing security and sustenance to a much larger population.

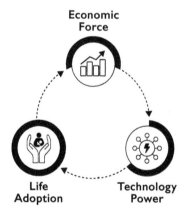

Economic Force

Life Adoption

Technology Power

The next big shift started around the 19th century. The Industrial Revolution, founded on technological disruptions of mechanisation and power, **changed the productivity of society** for the next 150 years, especially in Europe and North America. As a direct consequence, it raised the standard of living across the Western world, with consistent (perhaps for the first time in recorded history) economic growth over two centuries.

While technology is the trigger, it is powerful economic revolutions that drive change

Their spread disrupts productivity, changes consumption habits and the "quality of life", with multifaceted effects that ripple through society.

As a contrast to the discussion on data and hard power, there is growing discussion on the new concept of **"soft power"**. For years the US exercised this power as almost the sole "soft power" through its exports of Music and Hollywood movies.

Now there are rivals. From Africa to China, Bollywood movies and music resonate as they address key issues faced by a new generation today. (The movie "3 idiots" realised global popularity as it spoke movingly of youth choosing the independence to break away from parental expectations.)

Similarly, Korean tele-novelas ("Crash landing near you", the Korean Romance TV serial is a global hit), and Mexican soap operas. These are all transcending national boundaries. And create huge new business opportunities.

A) The advent of technology often enables different and better goods and services than could be imagined before. And new goods and services change the way we live, like electricity did in the 20th century. In many ways, **technology through economic changes helps re-imagine how we consume and how we live**.

B) Economic progress allows us to scale Maslow's hierarchy of human needs. As fundamental survival needs are taken care of, expressive or self actualisation needs come to the surface.

John Adams famously wrote in his letters, 'I must study politics and war, that our sons may have liberty to study mathematics and philosophy . . . in order to give right to their children to study painting, poetry, music'.

Economic prosperity generates the surplus for society that liberates us to explore intellectual or artistic pursuits. And these interests and creations travel across borders to create "soft power" (see box).

C) Highlighting the extensive effect of economic change, Friedrich Engels, in "The Condition of the Working Class" in England in 1844 spoke of "an industrial revolution, a revolution which at the same time changed the whole of civil society". The idea of a new social order based on major industrial change was clear even to writers like Charles Dickens.

Disruptive shifts in the structure of our economy shape our society, its habitats, its institutions, and in many ways, our very concept of mankind. Human habitation and civilisation developed initially with the shift to agriculture. Large-scale urbanisation evolved from the spread of the Industrial Revolution. And the domino effects of urbanisation, in itself, lead to transformative changes in human society.

These transformative changes, created by economic shifts, ripple through our world, creating countless opportunities for enterprise. (In subsequent chapters, we will look at some of the big structural societal shifts like urbanisation.)

5. THE SURGE IN THE SOUTH + A TRANSFORMATION BY TECHNOLOGY

The surge we see today in the South is, in a sense, still the ef
revolution that drove growth across Europe and North America ..
centuries. In this instance, it is accelerated by the speed with which ideas, ⎣aₚ
and goods travel in the modern world, and is amplified by the large weight of
populations who benefit.

Today, we stand at the cusp of yet **another series of disruptive changes** driven
by emerging technology – a digital revolution which could potentially reshape
the economy and re-imagine our lives much as electricity did in the past century:

- **Technological innovation will drive long-term gains in efficiency and productivity across every facet of enterprise and human activity.**

- **Entirely new ways will evolve to serve existing and new needs, with new products that deliver benefits that could not be thought of earlier. Delivering new pleasures and reducing chores.**

- **A disruption of the fabric of our economy and lives by technology will likely change future patterns of economic growth and consumption dramatically and reshape every aspect of daily lives.**

- **Rapid economic growth, with resulting social and consumption changes, will raise income levels and standards of living.**

This new "digitally driven" economic transformation is still in its infancy. As
the digital revolution gathers strength, its transformative impact will be more
widespread and faster than in the past.

And in the developing world, as the tech revolution combines with the economic "surge of the South", a much bigger wave of transformation will unfold.

The revolutions are becoming shorter; never before have two (powerful) revolutions been so closely interwoven. The resulting shifts in lifestyles and economies could be exponential.[2] Our economy is fundamentally changing, yet again.

NOTES

1 For centuries, the global economy was dominated by China and (undivided) India, which
together comprised 50% of the global economy. Some interesting snippets:

> Thanks to dedicated historians, humanity has access to Roman senate discussions.
> Apparently, a theme which often came up was the concern over the outflow of Gold
> and Silver ("Foreign Exchange") to China and India, to pay for manufactured goods
> like Calico or Porcelain, as well as raw materials like spices.

> A similar concern in England led to the East India Company being set up. Colonisation (through wars of conquest) took care of the trade imbalance with India. But it

took Opium exports (backed by the Opium wars between England/France and imperial China) to solve the trade imbalance with China . . . seen by today's standards both actions are reprehensible.

2 In part II of the book, we take a focus on the big pivots of technological disruption to understand the impact and opportunities in this tumult of change.

Chapter 3

Tumult of Age Pyramids

The Emerging Demographic Dividends

A key driver of economies and societies has been population growth and size. Indeed, the last centuries have seen an explosion of human population, driving and shaping the evolution of enterprise and societies.

Now, however, we see distinct changes in the profile of human population and growth. This chapter will examine the dramatic and disruptive changes happening to our demographics.

We will go beyond data to look at the implications for enterprise, of an ageing Europe, a plateauing Asia, and a booming Africa.

BACKGROUND: DEMOGRAPHICS AS A KEY DRIVER OF ECONOMIES AND ENTERPRISE

On the face of it, for global population to grow from an estimated 7 billion today to about 10 billion people by 2050 is good news for the economy.

The 20th century saw **human population grow explosively,** despite two world wars, from around 1.6 billion in the year 1900 to over 6 billion in the year 2000. Throughout this last century, and the ones preceding, demographic growth remained a key growth driver of economies. One which created several new business opportunities.

On the flip side, when the Black Death between 1347 and 1353 killed an estimated 20 million people in Europe, it lead to economic stagnation and recession over the next several decades.

Today as we forecast global population rising to, by some estimates, 10 billion humans by the year 2050, what does this portend for economic opportunities for enterprise? In this chapter we try and tease out the business implications that arise.

The one key assumption we make is that there will be no large natural disasters in the near term. Like the Toba Volcanic eruption 78,000 years ago, that according to recent studies, probably wiped out the Neanderthals and Denisovans!

(Though not without concerns on the environmental impact, which we talk about in Chapter 6.)

Within this overall growth, however, there are three key sub-trends we should take notice of:

DOI: 10.4324/9781003254737-4

1. Geographic dispersion

An ageing Europe, a plateauing Asia, and a booming Africa

The 20th century saw dramatic growth in human populations across the world, driven largely by improved health care and declining infant mortality. Asia, in particular, was a significant driver of population growth, prompting governments in China and India to resort to centralised family planning.

In recent years (see the following box), however, the significant slowdown in birth rates, caused by improved education and economic emancipation of women, has driven down birth rates sharply. The "Baby Boomers" generation, which caused the population bulge and economic growth for the last six decades, has now reached the age of retirement, and the next generation is not nearly as numerous.

Already, the population of **Europe** has stagnated at 730 million for the last few decades and is projected to decline slightly to 700 million by 2050. Global birth rates in 2015 (ref: "Our world in data" website) are at 1.61 children per woman – substantially lower than the "replacement levels" of 2.1 children per woman.

The average age of the population in Europe (Wikipedia) will rise from 37 years in 2003 to 51 years in 2050. And there will be four workers to support every two retirees. . . .

Not only does this mean (pension funds and) retirement plans will be hugely stressed, it also means working age populations will see a sustained and significant decline.

Continued support of ageing populations in developed countries may depend on large-scale immigration.

> **AN AGEING EUROPE, PLATEAUING ASIA AND A BOOMING AFRICA**
>
> Global population growth rates peaked at 2.1% in the 1960's and have declined steadily ever since, to under 0.2% p.a. today. This is driven by improving health care, and education and economic emancipation of women. **See section 2 below.**
>
> Looking forward, a Lancet study published in July 2020, has the **following highlights** which differ from traditional forecasts:
>
> World population is expected to peak in 2064 at around 9.7 billion and decline to 8.8 billion by 2100.
>
> By 2100, declining fertility rates in 183 countries (out of 195) will mean immigration is the only way they can maintain population levels and working age populations.
>
> Dramatic declines in working age populations may impact economic growth rates, even in China and India.
>
> This will lead to a significant shift in relative population weights of regions, with a resulting impact on economic opportunities for enterprise. Africa and the Middle East will lead growth in the youth demographic and working age populations, though even they will see declines in birth rates.

This will have interesting ramifications for local politics when the choice is between "economic decline and lower living standards" or "higher rates of immigration". . . .

Similarly, **Asia's** population growth is expected to slow, moving from 4.6 billion humans today to 5.3 billion people in 2050. This, along with the decline in working-age populations, may mean a significant slowdown in economic growth rates for several key economies in Asia.

Two-thirds of the foreseen population growth in this century will come from Africa and the Middle East. This is the next big growth opportunity for enterprise in the 21st century. . . .

2. Tumult of age pyramids

Asia will grow old before it grows rich. . . . Societies are ageing faster than we realise, turning the traditional demographic age pyramid upside down. What are the opportunities this provides for enterprise?

For as long as we can remember or record, human society has always been defined by a very well-structured age pyramid. A few old people, some middle-aged people, several young people, and lots of children. Most business opportunities were built around large numbers of children and growing populations.

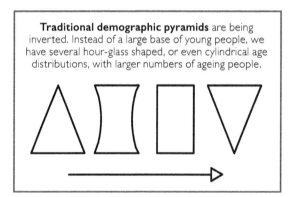

Traditional demographic pyramids are being inverted. Instead of a large base of young people, we have several hour-glass shaped, or even cylindrical age distributions, with larger numbers of ageing people.

With sudden, unforeseen mortality through disease or accident being common (and without good medical care, in many instances), the historical norm was to have large families. Partly as an insurance policy. And partly as an old-age-care insurance system.

With improving health care, we have seen a steep decline in birth rates. According to Wikipedia, population growth rates, which peaked in the year 1968 at 2.1%, have since dropped to 1.1% and could drop to zero by the end of this century.

The peak absolute number of babies born in any one year for mankind, on the other hand, was achieved in the year 2010, with an estimated 145 million new babies born in that year. Since then, each year has seen the number of babies born drop by an estimated million.

In countries like China (where the "one child" policy meant sharply lower birth rates), fewer children meant a generation of "little emperors" (single children with two doting parents and four grandparents). This, in turn, meant that the market for children's products (food, toys, clothing, schooling, etc.) saw accelerated growth of the "premium" segment.

Large parts of the world today are already at birth rates which are below "replacement levels" of 2.1 children per woman. (This is a statistical number. Of course, no one is expected to have 0.1 babies!!)

Only sub-Saharan Africa, the "Stans", and eastern India still have birth rates higher than this level.

A clear correlation seems to exist between economic development, quality of health care, and female emancipation, on the one hand, with the number of children and the size of families, on the other.

Human population, however, continues to grow, simply because people are not dying at the previous rate. Life expectancy is increasing. And therefore, the traditional demographic pyramid is getting challenged. In Japan, for instance, 25% of the population is above the age of 65. In China, some 300 million people are above the age of 60 – almost a quarter of the population – mainly because of the one child policy instituted in the 1980s.

Throughout history, most of our institutions and businesses have been catering to a young population base. Witness the large number of schools. And the space devoted in supermarkets and department stores to children's and young people's clothing. The ubiquity of young people in advertisements promoting products also has an effect.

As a result, we must look at the world using multiple lenses.

THREE DISTINCT DEMOGRAPHIC DIVIDENDS ARE EMERGING, EACH WITH A DISTINCT PROFILE OF CONSUMPTION:

A) **Societies where the traditional profile with a large number of young children and a demographic dividend of "working age populations" is forecast to continue well into the next several decades.**

A quick look at the shopping aisles in most supermarkets will reveal that one of the largest segment of shelf space is devoted to infant diapers. This directly reflects a largely young population with growing numbers of babies.

Throughout Africa and South Asia, the conventional "young people" lens still holds.

Similarly with working age populations and young adults growing in number, there will be a rise in the premium leisure industry. Whether it is luxury wear or holidays.

And therefore, established marketing patterns developed for Asia and the Americas over the last few decades will still hold. Market needs, segment sizes, and even shopping aisle allocations will be driven by a largely young population (see box).

Even in the entertainment industry, witness the growth of the global phenomenon, the Korean boy band BTS, catering primarily to pre teen kids. They have an annual revenue of a few billion dollars! This is a great example of an enterprise focused on the youth market.

At the same time, these young people will have changing outlooks and needs driven by the compounding effects of technological and economic change discussed in part II of this book.

Organisations which seek to cater to these markets will need to be agile in tracking and responding to these fast-evolving consumers.

B) **The second lens is one where the demographic pyramid has become a demographic cylinder, if not an "inverted pyramid" already.**

For the rest of the world, the lens has to now shift to something new. One that caters to the needs of older adults. Often retired and with plenty of leisure time and disposable income on their hands.

It is interesting to look at societies like Japan in this context (see box).

Although the India market still has a youth bulge forecast for the next two decades, better health care means there is an existing market of 100 million adults over the age of 65 – a large number in absolute terms!

And enterprise is stepping up to cater to their needs.

Health care, religion, meditation, yoga, adult diapers, tourism. . . . It is a new and fast-growing market with distinct needs that is often missed by traditional marketers focused on youth.

Adult grooming becomes very important for people who look for companionship in their senior years and thereby creates a completely new category of consumers.

In India, we see the emergence of old-age communities, "retirement homes", and "retirement villages" (at various price points) and special, older-adult community activities (cities like Mumbai have seen groups of retirees come together to organise community activities like cricket games!).

> **Japan** is one of the fastest ageing societies in our world. Already today, 25% of the population is over the age of 65. It is forecast that this number will rise to 40% by mid century. No wonder Japanese companies invest so heavily in automation and robotics!!
>
> As they age, many of these (retired) older people suffer from depression and sarcopenia (loss of muscle mass) caused by malnutrition.
>
> This is mainly driven by loneliness as these people are deprived of the social network at work.
>
> No wonder the country has created a **"Minister of Loneliness"**.
>
> Japan offers a live case study to benchmark economic and social opportunities for businesses in other countries as societies age.

A lot of this is driven also by migration (of the young adults to the US/elsewhere) and the resulting breakdown of the earlier social contract, whereby the young looked after their parents.

The more affluent retirees the world over drive global tourism and travel. Cruise ships are often a favourite. The travel industry would do well to take note of this changing demographic profile and tailor offerings to them. Whether it is in the seat and "leg-room" design or on the design of facilities and activities.

Similarly, we see the almost exponential growth of **medical tourism.** Bumrungrad hospital in Thailand was one of the first to identify this opportunity, accredit its doctors and facilities with insurance agencies in Europe and the US, and drive a very successful, multi-billion-dollar medical tourism industry. We now see several hospitals in India and other countries scramble to design their own offerings.

The ageing population also affects the design of technology-based products and services. From services that track whether the person has had a fall to helping create support groups for diabetes or other NCD, ageing is a huge, global emerging opportunity with distinct needs.

C) **The unlocking of women's economic potential:**

Women have always played a key role in traditional economies driven by agrarian handicrafts and agriculture. However, this contribution has not always been recognised or valued in economic terms.

Around the mid 90's, **Unilever** had a great marketing success with the launch of **"Dove"** soap and beauty care products targeted at women in their 40s. This was a huge success, and the company used real women from this target group (rather than young models).

In doing so, the company was recognising that **baby boomers** who had formed a **key demographic** for their growth over the years, were now ageing and with distinct needs.

In general though, marketers have long recognised the role of the woman in driving purchase decisions within the household, and most marketing is targeted at them. In an earlier era, this was in their role as homemakers. Increasingly it is in their role as independent, confident professionals.

As women around the world step out of their traditional roles, enabled by improved social understanding and legal frameworks that support their move, this demographic is key to emerging economic opportunities.

We discuss this aspect more in Chapter 6 on institutions and will not devote much time here, except to note that this is a key demographic which will shape buying decisions based on their evolving lifestyles. And will likely create several opportunities for enterprise.

3. Beyond numbers: shaping "how we think"

The impact of demographic changes on our thinking and attitudes will continue to evolve as societies are re-shaped.

Consider people's expectations of their economic prospects for themselves and their children. We see a stark difference across geographies.

Most people in the "developed" countries are generally pessimistic about the future, while most emerging markets are very optimistic about the future.

This is perhaps at least partly driven by their direct experiences over the last few decades: whether their economies are growing fast (like in Asia) or are stagnating

(Japan, Europe). It is perhaps also linked to security of income and employment. And of course, ageing.

Inevitably, though, attitudes towards the future shape spending patterns, consumption patterns, levels of indebtedness, and the attitude towards business.

Similarly, opportunities for migration discussed earlier in this chapter will only compound and muddle the change in the markets where people migrate out from, especially as migrants will feed back to their societies attitudes, consumption patterns, expectations, and learnings from the societies they have migrated to.

An example is the Indian state of Kerala, where large numbers of migrants to the Middle East have re-shaped local real estate, housing, health care, and even politics.

A closing thought. . . .

We should therefore resist getting drawn into thinking of demographics as either static or linear. Our growth rates and age pyramids are highly volatile and respond to changing circumstances, including economics, health care, or even natural disasters.

Enterprises must be sensitive to emerging demographic niches as they evolve. Identify the changing demographic patterns in our market. Understand them deeply to get insights about their unmet needs. And then modify our business paradigms and institutional paradigms to cater to these unmet needs. This will often require a period of experimentation, trial, and error, before one hits upon the successful model.

This has profound implications for business and marketers, as well as for social institutions. It also presents a huge business opportunity if we can identify these niches early and differentiate our offerings and business models for each segment.

Chapter 4
The Surge of Urbanisation
Transformation by Habitat

*For the first time in history, over 50% of humanity lives in cities. Africa and Asia are urbanising **at a furious pace**. What is this change; why is this important for the world of enterprise? And what opportunities will it create?*

I. THE BIG SHIFT – URBANISATION OF THE SOUTH

One of the big shifts playing out today is the unprecedented urban surge in the South

Asia, which was predominantly rural, is now rapidly evolving to become predominantly urban. A similar shift can be seen rippling across Africa with cities like Lagos, Cairo, and Nairobi.

At the turn of the 18th century, only 3% of the world was urban. This increased dramatically over the last two centuries, and since 2018, for the first time in human history, over half the human population now lives in cities or urban areas.

In the next five years, Asia is expected to reach this "tipping point". Asian cities already account for half the world's urban population and are expected to contribute the bulk of growth in global urban populations over the next decade.

The largest cities today are now in the Third World

Seven of the ten most populous "mega cities" (cities with population in excess of 10 million) are now in Asia. The Greater Delhi area – an urban area of 28 million in 2020 – is expected to grow to be the largest urban agglomeration in the world by 2030.

Similar surges are to be seen in Jakarta, Manila, and elsewhere. Large cities are surging in population, swallowing surrounding areas. As transformed urban centres, they are changing the shape of nations and that of the world.

DOI: 10.4324/9781003254737-5

2. URBANISATION: A PIVOT OF TRANSFORMATION

Man has changed his habitat several times. Originating as hunter-gatherers, people moved to an agrarian existence for many centuries and then shifted towards a town- and city-centred existence. **These shifts were breakpoints which redefined societies and the way we live**. The human habitat is a dominant marker of who we are. Changes affect a wide variety of issues, including governance, culture, social structures, and more.

What underpins urban evolution, its form and scale? Urban planners, social scientists, and developmental economists provide us with an understanding of the changes happening now. We build on this to identify implications for the world of enterprise and economic action.

3. BEYOND THE NUMBERS: CHARACTERISTICS OF URBANISATION AND THE EVOLUTION OF CITIES

The earliest cities were **enabled by habitability**. They came into existence as humanity shifted from a nomadic "hunter-gatherer" lifestyle to an agrarian one dependent on farming and creating surpluses that allowed larger settlements to flourish.

Such settlements were often close to water sources, such as rivers and lakes, and slowly expanded to form the seeds of the first "cities".

Over time, urban areas have come to be characterised by a density of human structures – houses, places of worship and work, and infrastructure like roads and bridges. But what is it that underpins this physical reality? What is it that makes our urban centres develop in their distinctive way?

We draw upon the work of social scientists to understand the evolution of cities. Paul Wheatly, in The Pivot of the Four Quarters (1971), emphasises the **cultural and societal role of cities**.

- The first urban forms emerged as **ritual/governance centres** through which they dominated surrounding regions with their sacred practices and authority. Often, religion and governance came together and combined with imperial administration. Temples or other sacred institutions dominated the skyline.

- Only later did financial institutions and trade enhance this societal role. **Mercantile cities** emerged, often built around powerful and wealthy merchants – cities which created wealth and capital by themselves instead of simply extracting a tithe from the rural agricultural hinterland. Land-based trade along the Silk Road and other maritime trading routes attracted and nurtured settlements. Often, these also became centres of political power.

- The commercial role and impact of cities progressively increased over time. Gideon Sjoberg highlighted the fact that cities became differentiated and developed on the **basis of the society's technological sophistication**.

Prior to the Industrial Revolution, artisanal skill and animal labour were the foundation for economic production.

Thereafter, **new technologies** from the Industrial Revolution enabled the emergence of new cities. These drew upon energy sources and mechanisation to expand productivity and become centres of technical and economic activity.

*   Enterprise and economic institutions are key to urban evolution.

A major force for urbanisation was the emergence of new sources of livelihoods which were not dependent on access to farming. Secondly, cities enabled a wider variety of services like education to emerge, transforming the quality of urban lives. This wide variety of available jobs and superior quality of life attracted people to cities.

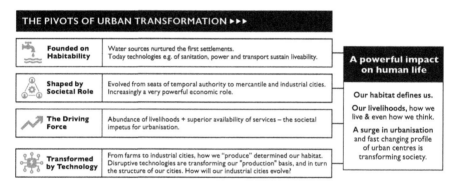

*   Faster means of transport and improved communication technologies enabled the transformation of urban settlements into the larger cities of today. New technologies and the possibility to transport people, goods, and information rapidly creates new opportunities for enterprise and development.

Where we live defines us, and the urban transformations have a powerful impact. Understanding the changes and the forces behind it enables us to seize the emerging opportunities.

4. WHAT ARE THE BIG CHANGES HAPPENING TODAY? WHAT ARE THE IMPLICATIONS AND OPPORTUNITIES?

A) The urban shift: a coalescing of multiple shifts

We have seen the accelerated urbanisation in Asia. From under 10% of the population in 1900 to almost 50% today. This surge in urban populations and the structure of urban agglomerations represents a very visible transformation. But this is not just a change in habitat or statistics. Underlying this shift is a transformation in the people and their lives – their incomes, occupations, lifestyles, consumption, needs, and much more. These coalesce to make the urbanisation change even more disruptive than a simple physical shift implies.

- **The Economic Surge:** Urbanisation has come with a growth in income through transition from agricultural jobs to industry and services. Recent growth has come due to expansion of the manufacturing and services sectors. Division of labour enabled productivity gains, and increased leverage of the human capital of creativity and knowledge is enabling a surge in real incomes.

- Transformed **demographic patterns and thinking** visibly enhances this change. Cities of the (economic) South today reflect their demographic youth bulge. Bangalore – India's IT epicentre, with its youthful population, education institutes, and cosmopolitan culture of cuisine and entertainment – is but one such example. Globalisation has transformed the values and culture of youth, and rapid income growth has accelerated adoption of Western consumption and lifestyles.

- A transformation of an archetypal rural society to an urban one. Delhi, Metro Manila, Jakarta, or the many mini-metros are driving the aspirations of nations today, even though many parts of their countries remain rural. Many of these countries are going through a turbulent period as this transformation gains momentum.

Understanding these social changes can drive opportunities for enterprise and development.

B) The rise of urban agglomerations

Cities have always been characterised as large, denser-populated settlements that buzz as social and economic ecosystems. Now, however, we see cities merging with each other to create mega urban agglomerations with implications beyond just population numbers. These agglomerations, or mega-cities, often span entire regions and create "urban corridors".

The Asian Development Bank (ADB) has highlighted the magnitude of some of these changes in Asia. This section draws substantially upon their work.

Asian mega-cities are forming. Mega-cities (ranging from Istanbul with 10 million to Tokyo with 36 million today) create large geographic sprawls that dominate and influence surrounding regions or even countries.

City-regions (in fact mega-regions!): Over the last couple of decades, mega-cities

expanded to engulf entire regions and smaller towns in their vicinities and sometimes merged with other such clusters and created entirely new, extended mega urban corridors, or regions. That extended way beyond their original geographic boundaries. This often creates comparative advantages of access and transport for enterprise and economic activity along this corridor.

The extended Bangkok region in Thailand is one such example that has extended over 200 kilometres from its original centre.

Some of these city regions are actually larger than smaller countries, like Belgium or the Netherlands, both in geographic area and population. These are often economic units in their own right.

Mega-regions already exist in North America and Europe and are now increasingly seen across Asia. The Tokyo-Nagoya-Osaka-Kyoto-Kobe mega-region hosts almost 40% of Japan's population. Similarly, the Hong Kong-Shenzhen-Guangzhou region is home to almost 120 million people! Clusters like these also tend to spur innovation in several areas, from urban governance to new services and products.

Urban corridors, on the other hand, are cities located at some distance from each other but coalesce as a single entity through transportation networks. They often link a number of city centres and mega-cities on a developmental axis with specific economic and transportation objectives, thereby leading to economic development across the region.

These stronger ties stimulate business, innovation, economic zones, and real estate values all along their linkages, creating extended economic zones.

An example is the developing Mumbai-Delhi corridor, which will stretch more than 1,500 km from JNPT (Navi Mumbai) to Tughlakabad in Delhi.

Similarly, one can look at the Klang Valley manufacturing/service corridor that stretches from Kuala Lumpur to port Klang. Or even the 1,500-km-long corridor that stretches from Beijing to Seoul and thence to Tokyo across four countries. Over 77 cities lie on this route, with a total population of almost 100 million!

These urban agglomerations tend to grow faster economically than the countries they are located in, in the process attracting even larger numbers of migrants. They are economic powerhouses with the typically large demographic concentrations, large captive markets in their own right, and with significant capabilities in technological innovation.

C) The rise of city-states: economic and societal powerhouses

With the urbanisation surge in the South, cities account for a disproportionate share of economic productivity. In Viet Nam, for instance, 30% of the population live in urban areas but contribute almost 70% of gross domestic product (GDP).

Similarly in the Philippines with Manila, or Indonesia with greater Jakarta, Bangladesh with Dhaka, or Pakistan with Karachi. In each case, these cities contribute disproportionately to GDP and carry significant economic and political clout within the respective countries. The top 120 cities in China account for 75% of GDP. Seoul is about half the country's GDP.

These emerging urban agglomerations have populations and economies larger than many countries, and indeed, they are "city-states" in all but name. Some are already city-states, like Singapore or Hong Kong, with a strong regional influence.

Many opportunities exist in these mega-cities, but a special focus is needed at the enterprise level to realise their potential. Their rapid scale necessitates a disproportionate build-up of infrastructure, leveraging technology.

> ## RISE OF THE CITY STATES & A NEW FOCUS ON THE URBAN.
>
> By 2050, urban populations will double to account for almost 70% of society. This shift will change governance as well as the way enterprise organises itself. We see **three change pivots emerging.**
>
> **1)** Governments have swivelled to prioritise an urban transformation with unprecedented infrastructure funds and a mission focussed approach. New forms of governance are evolving to provide greater focus and administrative autonomy to these city states, veritable nations in themselves.
>
> **2)** Critical roles are emerging also for international institutions like the world bank, to promote inclusive and sustainable development as new capabilities will be required in urban planning and development on this mega scale.
>
> **3)** Equally enterprise is reorganising structures, products and selling systems to cater to the city states. Not only are these the largest economic opportunities, they are seeing unprecedented change in competition and consumers alike.

Governments must formulate policies that nurture the growth of such regions to their maximum transformative potential, with innovation in local government and institutions.

D) Urban problems

The outsize economic weight of these regions notwithstanding, they are also often beset with a host of problems, ranging from high real estate prices, poor quality of air and environment, and traffic congestion, leading to lower quality of life.

The demands of their large populations outstrip available space in a constrained geographic spread. High land prices drive the population into slums forming in a Mumbai, Manila, Rio, or Lagos.

Several businesses then move to the peripheries. Long commuting times of even a couple of hours each way are common. Efficient high-speed rail networks have often lagged behind these areas' explosive growth.

Mind-numbing jams on city roads, long delays, air and noise pollution become the defining characteristic of most of these mega-regions. They can affect the economy and "quality of life" negatively, with people forced to endure long commutes to work in boring, repetitive, low-skilled jobs. Safe water supply, electricity, and sewage disposal systems often come under severe strain in these populations.

URBAN CHALLENGES-OPPORTUNITIES FOR DOING GOOD & DOING WELL.

Infrastructure is the most pressing need with the urban surge. An opportunity to finance and create transportation systems, housing, and fundamental services like water, electricity and sanitation. The world bank estimates the global need for urban infrastructure at $4.5-5.4 trillion, with the largest part of it in developing countries.

Environment is another challenge which is coming to the fore. Cities account over 70% of greenhouse gas emissions (and energy consumption). In Delhi, Beijing, and many other large Asian centres, "severe" air quality days are worrying. Solutions for controlling pollution and more sustainable living are prime opportunities.

Cities are at the epicentre of **new challenges.** The covid crisis impacted the largest cities the most, and called upon the resourcefulness of healthcare workers and administrators to innovate with speed and resilience...

New **smart city solutions** are emerging using digital technology to manage resources more efficiently and deliver superior benefits in a sustainable way. Data based managements of street lights and transport system are just a small example. **New disaggregated systems** are reaching out to the underprivileged. Jalodbust, a start up in India, seeks to provide mobile sanitation services to houses not connected to a sewage system.

Such challenges are opportunities for enterprises, governments, NGOs, and citizens alike.

E) The urban poor

Slums, which are home to urban poor, are a common sight across several such urban mega-clusters. Almost 11% of youth in Asian clusters are unemployed. Often, young people are much more likely than older people to be unemployed.

Illustrative are the **triumphs and tribulations of any typical urban Asian metro**; it is a dynamic city with exemplary economic growth. The apparel industry is a large employer and boasts global supply chains, attracting several ancillary suppliers of goods and services. However, the city is also witness to large slums, traffic congestion, water shortages (only a quarter have piped water at home), poor quality of sanitation (only 9% of households have access to sanitation and often have to walk long distances to get access to a public toilet), and serious breakdowns of law and order. Slums are often in low-lying, flood-prone areas.

And it is similar in a Lagos, Mumbai, Dhaka, Manila. . . .

A few decades ago, CK Prahlad's seminal work bought into focus the economic opportunity at the bottom of the pyramid, despite these problems. The problems of the poor in the new urban centres also represents a transformation opportunity for enterprise, government, and NGOs alike.

5. THE RISE OF POST-INDUSTRIAL CITIES

Even as the surge of urbanisation transforms our world, a second and even more powerful wave is starting to build. Rapid advances in technology are transforming the very paradigm of urban living.

- New technologies can alter the way cities address urban issues; for example, that of transportation, sanitation, and pollution. Technology is enabling very different solutions to city problems, and hence, changing the cities themselves.

- Most of all, technology and the digital world is re-shaping the way citizens work, play, and live, changing the very DNA and structure of our cities.

Once again, we may see technology power a dramatic transformation in our economies, societies, and even in the nature of our cities. We could see new post-industrial habitats that reflect a shift from an industrial era to digitally powered economies with a greater emphasis on service and knowledge.

Perhaps even a reshaping of urban agglomeration – a shift towards dispersed settlements but energised with strong digital connectivity.

Where we live shapes our society and lives. Embedded in our transforming habitats are big, new opportunities for enterprise as well as governments.

Chapter 5
What We Think
Transformation by Belief

"We are what we think, all that we are arises with our thoughts, with our thoughts we make the world."

– Gautam Buddha

We explore the power of thought and belief – in "How We Think" – and how it is disruptively impacting the world. The way in which our attitudes have evolved and are still evolving. And in how this affects enterprise.

Here, we focus much more on the intangible than the tangible. A shift from looking at economic revolutions, urbanisation, and population shifts to looking at thoughts and beliefs. The mind versus the material!

Ideas are the energy that trigger change.

Powerful technology ideas are indeed palpably re-shaping our world. However, our ideas of what we value and think are just-as-powerful drivers of change.

Historically, the wildfire-spread of religions, and in later centuries, the Renaissance, demonstrates the power of ideas and thought. And its impact on how we live is a most visible example of how beliefs shape our actions and all aspects of society.

We see **emerging trends** in consumer attitudes and behaviours. Alternative living, a connected world, consumerism and anti-consumerism! Consumers start to make choices of the company whose products they buy based on how the company **"behaves"**. Investors follow suit and reward them with capital. What does this mean for enterprise, and how should one respond?

Leveraging **"what we think"** can be an opportunity for enterprise.

I. FUNDAMENTAL FORCES SHAPE WHAT WE VALUE – DRIVE CHANGE IN OUR EVERYDAY LIVES AND BUSINESSES

Trends, or emerging patterns of how we live and work, shape the world of enterprise in a variety of ways. From transitory fads that create "shooting star

DOI: 10.4324/9781003254737-6

opportunities" to longer-term fashion and style trends, and even megatrends and enduring shifts that drive business success over longer time horizons.

Here, we look at three fundamental forces that are ascendant today – values and beliefs that will drive our preferences.

A) The mainstreaming of Gaia

Witness the growth of local, artisanal, organic food brands driven by Millennials. The growth of "Naked" stores. Millennials now look for companies that help heal the environment, going beyond "not polluting".

What vivifies this powerful belief space best is the Gaia concept. Various cultures traditionally believed that they were part of a larger community of life that included sky, water, air, soil, and fire, representing a fundamental kinship amongst the living and inanimate. They possessed a respect for the primordial and the organic life force, with an eye on sustaining this life-force.

The British scientist James Lovelock crystallised this as a scientific idea called "Gaia", after the Greek Goddess of Earth, resonating the belief that Earth was alive and that we are a part of her life.

Organic foods, sustainability, and conservation draw upon roots similar to this metaphor of Gaia. Big movements to save the planet, 'Green' thinking, and other related streams have captured the imagination of today's world.

NATURALS SUSTAINABILITY **GAIA** GREEN THINKING ALT LIVING COMMUNITY ORGANIC LIFE PRIMORDIAL **KINSHIP** CONSERVATION FORCE RENEWABLE

This confluence of beliefs, sometimes grouped as a way of alt living, are no longer just the passion of a select few. Today it is the mainstream perception, even in the developing world (see the "Chipko" movement[1]) – the desired way to live on Earth.

What makes this disruptive is its omnipresence and power. The mainstreaming of Gaia is a world force that is driving our lives, businesses, governance, and politics and even our quest for new technologies.

Personal consumption brands show the most visible impact of the growing importance of this theme. The food industry especially has embraced Gaia with organic foods, vegan diets, and a return to ancestral grains like millets or quinoa.

To mediate the conflict between conservation and consumption, Gaia beliefs are spurring powerful new technologies – effluent treatments, micro-irrigation, tug boats to clean the plastic patch in the oceans . . . and many, many more. Powerful, new technologies are anchoring transformative businesses, new supply chains, and many other forms of opportunity for enterprise. Renewable energy investments today are at 28% of fresh investments in energy. EVs today are slowly but surely taking over transportation, whether it be buses, two-wheelers, cars, or trains.

Often seen as just the soul of artisanal brands, today, the mainstreaming of Gaia is compelling large businesses to adopt such beliefs as central to their corporate "*raison d'être*".

Not merely restricted to individual activity, environmental beliefs are transforming the body politic of our world, compelling the adoption of high-profile, defining international pacts like the COP26.

Gaia is becoming a foundational belief shaping the way individuals make their choices. It is disrupting the actions of companies, investors, innovators, and nations at a fundamental level.

B) The upheaval of uncertainty

The headlines of turbulence besiege us: global warming, fires, and floods. Economic upheavals; instability of nations and their finances. A bewildering range of newness; contentious political strife. Job losses and illnesses sweeping out from nowhere.

Professor Galbraith's seminal work in 1973 captioned the emerging times as the "Age of Uncertainty" to reflect the sharp contrast between the great

certainties in "19th-century economy" and the much less assured reality of the "market-oriented economies" of the 20th century.

Alvin Toffler, the futurist, in his visionary book *Future Shock* (1970), presaged the disruptive impact of modern digital and communication technologies and coined the title. He highlighted "the impact of new environments coming at you, and coming rapidly" and the challenges to society as it engages with rapid technological and cultural change.

Today, we are seeing more change than ever before. Tofleresque future shocks are arriving with an increasing frequency. Disruptive technologies are re-imagining our world and driving economic upheavals. In an increasingly flat and connected world, change and upheavals such as these arrive more frequently and with increased unpredictability. Accentuated political conflicts, the shadows of terrorism, climate change events, and the globally paralysing Covid pandemic seem to define a new normal of an uncertain world.

In this epoch of disruption, the former military term VUCA (Volatile, Uncertain, Complex, Ambiguous) is a defining characteristic of our times.

The upheaval of uncertainty changes the way people think and act, altering our willingness to take risks. We adopt a far lesser deterministic world view of life than in the past, and it affects our minds and behaviours in two divergent ways:

- On one hand, consumers want to cocoon themselves and live in worlds insulated from the turbulence. Established "brands" leverage this appeal and offer tranquillity and familiar comfort. The product appeal of "savings and insurance" is becoming universal. A "back to roots" movement is seeing the revival of traditional foods, customs, even religions.

- On the other hand, consumers, in particular the younger set, who have grown up in this age of turbulence, embrace the change and seek out the opportunities within it. They adroitly cruise the change, searching for new products and adopting lifestyles built around the acceptance of uncertainty. Continuous learning is built into their DNA and they are at comfort with technological disruption.

Not only individuals but enterprises, organisations, and governments are also impacted by this new reality. The explosive growth of start-ups and a "mindset of risk-taking" illustrate how businesses are seizing opportunity by cruising the change. In many ways, this is the biggest transformation in the world of business.

The Age of Uncertainty has truly arrived and is a powerful force shaping our world. "How does the upheaval of uncertainty change the way our enterprise operates and the opportunities we see", is one of the most important questions for us to answer in our role as "change leaders".

C) Consumerism: a farewell to frugality; a path to progress

Yuval Noah Harari, in his book *Sapiens*, refers to consumerism as perhaps the fastest growing religion on earth, with adherents in every society.

The economic surge in the South has brought to the fore a new avatar of consumerism. People are trying to secure the advantages of modern living for themselves by consuming more convenience products and services and by using their lifestyle to "define" themselves.

Consumerism is seen as a path to progress (and not a mere hedonistic excess or an indulgence in wasteful consumption).

Consumerism is fuelling a rapid build-up of markets and economies, establishing new standards of health and education and providing the energy for upward mobility. It is a key driver for innovation and technology development.

A large market opportunity is unlocked by consumers saying a "farewell to frugality" as a mind-set, though inevitably, they are still constrained by their means.

2. THE EMERGENCE OF NEW BELIEFS

The power of our thoughts and ideas shapes our world. And in a world of change, our ideas evolve continuously. Indeed, there are powerful new streams emerging of "what we think". Also, significant changes are taking place in how new thoughts and values form and take root in society.

• The new global: "Thoughts R Us"

Driven by trade, power, and plunder, the Imperialistic Age (around the middle of the last millennium) saw a connecting of the world across the seven seas. Thereafter, global supplies, triggered by the efficiencies of the Industrial Revolution, evolved into today's integrated global supply chain.

Today, the world is stepping beyond these physical linkages. The new global is the global of "thought". Ideas and experiences are flowing across the globe with unprecedented intensity and speed.

Spurred on by a connected world and a breaking of barriers (e.g., the everyday use of translators!), the global melting pot today has wings. Individuals have access to a world of thoughts and are increasingly driven by them.

> **HOW IDEAS ARE SHAPING TODAY**
>
> 1) **The new global of thoughts, ideas and beliefs** flowing across the world, at twitter speed
>
> 2) **A universe of microcosms:** Narrow focussed belief groups with adherents across the world
>
> 3) **Influencers shape ideas:** The micro messiahs of today

Even in the work environment and in business organisations, "global and cross-national" teams are now the norm, and this further accelerates the exchange and flow of attitudes, thoughts, and ideas.

Business ideas migrating across nations provide new opportunities. WeChat from China was one of the first communication apps that offered seamless cash transfers. This feature has now spread across the world.

• A universe of microcosms

Even as the world homogenises, an equally strong counter-force is emerging. A rising assertion of "individuality", by actively resisting a global uniformity.

Witness the rise of strong political action groups or the emerging, powerful segmentation in the markets of today. These microcosms are baby universes of opportunity for distinctive products and services for business success as well as for political parties to build their foundation for overall success.

Though this may seem like **anti-globalisation**, these microcosms, while bound by a narrower group's focus, have adherents beyond boundaries. These are the global Facebook "groups" and tribes of today.

• The new fountainhead of thoughts

Powerful ideas historically have had their origins in thought leaders, messiahs, economic messiahs, and more, spreading with missionary zeal, religions of faith, or even religions of economic practice like Marxism.

Today, we are seeing a dis-aggregation. It's a world of **multiple "influencers"** shaping thoughts, preferences, and actions. Often using social media. And even moulding everyday life choices. They are today's micro-messiahs.

Increasingly, beliefs are also emerging not from a single thought leader but from the bubbling up of the beliefs of millions of individuals. Coalescing into powerful movements, they form the institutions of change, or change the institutions of today. Hash tags and political waves resonate in our world every day.

Movements seem to form spontaneously, take root, and spread with a frequency like never before. Witness the Arab Spring.

3. LEVERAGING THE POWER OF BELIEF

At a time when societal change is high and disruptions are reshaping markets, the forecasting of trends and mega-trends has significantly grown in importance. Business, societies, governments, and industries are increasingly demanding insights into future developments. Trendspotting, practices, and tools are helping businesses to pick out and act in them.

In fact, a McKinsey study emphasises that riding longer-term industry and geographic trends is a pivotal contributor to business results – a company benefiting from such tailwinds is more likely to rise to the top of future performers. Indeed, "The trend is your friend".

And, as we look at the varied shifts impacting our world and businesses, we wish to reinforce the power of "what we think". Making sense – and making use – of our beliefs, the foundational forces of change will help envision and shape markets to one's advantage.

NOTE

1 Chipko movement, also called Chipko andolan, was a non-violent social and ecological movement by rural villagers – particularly women – in India in the 1970s, aimed at protecting trees and forests slated for government-backed logging. The Hindi word chipko means "to hug" or "to cling to" and reflects the demonstrators' primary tactic of embracing trees to impede loggers (www.britannica.com).

Such movements are resonating throughout the world, often reflecting a confluence of belief, economic realities, environmental events, and an assertion of rights by indigenous people.

Chapter 6

Society and Its Institutions

Unbundling and Re-creation

In the previous chapter, we looked at how individual attitudes are being re-shaped. In this chapter, we will focus on institutions because they serve as a vehicle whereby we transmit (and possibly even amplify) a legacy of beliefs and behaviours, with impact that lasts beyond any single individual's or organisation's lifespan.

*Social institutions enable the **codification of beliefs into "rules and rituals" to influence the implementation of the belief systems.** They shape everyday life and societal expectations and are also the foundation that underpins corporate and legal institutions.*

*Businesses look for the strength of institutions in society to ensure good governance. Good **institutions provide predictability of laws and level playing fields,** which allows business to invest with a reasonable expectation of return. Equally, business opportunities resonate with the codes of everyday life influenced by societal institutions.*

*Now, **traditional institutions are being unbundled and recreated** as economic pendulums swing and as technology enables the re-structuring of traditional value chains.*

Each of these changes is disruptive in itself and is an opportunity for enterprise to re-imagine value chains and create new capabilities to establish competitive advantage. We will look at how this change affects the economy and creates new business opportunities.

WELCOME TO THE BRAVE NEW WORLD!

Several institutions have shaped society over millennia and contributed to the evolution of society and business as we know it. We will examine how five key sets of institutions (see the following box) are changing and what this means for business.

- Of primary social groups – our families

- Of belief systems – our religions. We also explore new emerging "belief systems" like consumerism and sustainability

DOI: 10.4324/9781003254737-7

- Of enterprise and corporations

- Of governance – national, international, and political/economic/corporate

- Of other institutions shaping life spaces, as perhaps in education (which we look at as a case study)

1. Institutions of primary social groups – our families

The family has been a key institution historically, establishing security, authority, social norms, and even transfer of family "skills".

In years past, people trained with their parents to be farmers, carpenters, masons, artists. . . . The family was the key social, economic, as well as educational institution.

Professional guilds were often controlled by key families and were a way to ensure succession of employment, lucrative monopolies, and cash flow, as well as to exclude competition.

Some of the key drivers of change here are: accelerating urbanisation and new economic models, as well as the impact of new ideas.

> To help us with the drivers of change in these institutions we borrow a framework from the Encyclopaedia Brittanica which explains social change as resulting from causal connections between two or more processes.
>
> They outline some of these processes that contribute to drive social change, such as:
>
> **Changes in the natural environment.** Caused by climate change, natural disasters or disease (for example, the Bubonic plague in the Middle Ages).
>
> **Changes arising from demographics.** We have discussed this in an earlier chapter.
>
> **Changes arising from technological innovation**
>
> **Changes arising from economic processes.** (Such as the changes that led to property rights evolving from "Feudal Lord-Peasant" to "Proprietor-Tenant" relationship. In Socialist societies like post-independence India, this further evolved to offer property rights directly to the tenants or "tillers of the land")
>
> **Changes arising from new "ideas", social movements or political processes.**

We see four distinct evolutions in this institution of the family, with a resulting impact on business.

A) From joint to nuclear to blended/single-parent family structures

Yuval Noah Harari has written in his books about how, over time, people have surrendered "familial" and "religious" authority to the "state" to recognise marriages, rule on inheritance, medical care, old-age care, or codes of acceptable social behaviour.

What was earlier the authority of the parent or *paterfamilias* is now increasingly devolved to the government, or the state. We see, for instance, how, in the area of education and skills transfer, the historical role of the family has eroded, with schools and other educational systems and institutions taking over. This enables children to move beyond their "inherited" profession.

And yet, the parental role in this area hasn't disappeared completely. Parents who devote time, particularly in pre-school years, see better academic and social performance of their children in school; children whose parents are university graduates are more likely to go to college themselves.

Similarly, with improving methods of contraception and the delinking of sex from pregnancy, the future of the marriage contract may evolve.

A key driver of consumer-focussed businesses in any society (indeed, we believe the consumer is the ultimate driver of all businesses, whether directly or indirectly), has been the rate of creation of new family households.

A new house means a new place to stay, new furnishings, new modern conveniences (refrigerator/ovens, cooking equipment and utensils, cleaning equipment, climate control devices like fans and so on).

The historical move away from joint families which were geographically concentrated, towards nuclear families which are highly mobile in search of employment opportunities has, over the last century, led to a boom in construction as well as consumption of durables as listed above.

Similarly, another change is in the **opportunity to re-define the brand of consumables** used inside the household. What toothpaste, which shampoo or soap, detergent powders, cosmetics, etc.

Once we grow up with a brand of toothpaste we remain remarkably loyal to this brand throughout life. Unless a change is driven by a new life partner choosing her brand as the "house brand".

Fragmentation and re-creation of family structures, for whatever reason, are key opportunities for business and brands.

An interesting thought experiment could be to forecast where this might lead to in the modern world as we see the rise of divorce rates, remarriages, and blended or single parent families.

The re-definition and unbundling of the historically sacred "marriage contract" as an institution may create several new opportunities, including child care services, ageing care services, insurance, health care models, financial sharing arrangements, new product opportunities, and so on.

As lifespans of marriages outlive the immediate biological cause of raising a family, an "unbundling" of this historically "sacred" contract might possibly occur.

Will a "marriage" contract be for a binding term, which involves the kids reaching majority, and then be open to dissolution? Will the state take an increasingly larger role in child care?

We already see the increasing role of the state in defining the limits of physical violence ("spare the rod and spoil the child" now belongs to a distant past), and in education, by defining standards, curriculum, and testing/certification.

All of this will have a profound impact on business, as the setting up of new family households has been a key driver for several businesses: real estate, construction, town planning, home appliances, and even consumables (see box).

B) Evolving gender roles and stereotypes

One of the implications of longevity, retirement, ageing, and health described in an earlier chapter is the shortage of young people in key jobs.

Driven partly by talent shortages and equally by an evolving understanding of the limitations of traditional gender stereotypes, an emerging theme is the increasing participation of women in formal employment, and changing gender stereotypes.

Women increasingly now participate equally in political processes and often head governments (India, Germany, New Zealand).

Even Saudi Arabia has seen these winds of change blow across the land, with women now being allowed to drive cars and run businesses. This creates new opportunities for business, even as it challenges previous paradigms.

The acceleration of "Work from Home" paradigms driven by Covid-19 has meant that women may possibly find it easier than earlier to balance family and work.

Whether in business, politics, or in the armed forces, we see women increasingly playing a part. Across almost all countries,

In emerging countries like Bangladesh, the high human development indices, as well as the successes of an NGO like BRAC or businesses like Grameen bank are directly because of their success in empowering and engaging women.

We increasingly see women as successful global company CEOs, creating a great role model for the next generation. This does however, require companies to be set up to harness diversity.

As has been argued (Reynolds and Lewis, Harvard Business Review), the most important trait we seek inside our teams, particularly in disruptive times, is a diversity of thinking styles: **cognitive diversity.** This helps look at new problems in a variety of different perspectives, thereby helping formulate a more robust response to change.

Gender, ethnicity and a varied skill set are good proxies to help create this. But this has to be consciously selected and nurtured.

And this has to be supported by creating a culture of psychological safety where this diversity feels safe, valued, and free to express its individuality.

Companies who are able to do this well, (and certainly we see good examples now in Silicon Valley and in startups across the globe) are well placed to deal with disruptive change.

fewer jobs continue to be an exclusive male preserve. New regulatory statutes and better enforcement of them increase the odds of equal opportunities. Though, of course, there is still quite a journey ahead of us before we can claim to have achieved "full" gender equality. But the trend is (hopefully) here to stay.

C) The emergence of "global families and tribes"

has been an unfolding trend, as people migrate in search of education, employment opportunities, or even to escape persecution. Look at some numbers to understand the sheer scale of the impact.

Almost 1 million Filipinos leave the country each year to live overseas. In a population of ~90 million people, overseas Filipinos are a population of almost 10 million and contribute via remittances (through official as well as unofficial channels) to about 20% of the country's GNP!!

Similarly, the Indian diaspora constitutes an estimated 35 million (Wikipedia and Website of the Ministry of External Affairs, Government of India, reporting "Non Resident Indians" with Indian passports and also persons of Indian origin with foreign passports). If one adds second- and third-generation Indian diaspora who are still connected culturally to their land of origin, this number could perhaps be significantly larger.

In total, this could be almost 3% of India's population. This means not only inward remittances and investments (according to World Bank reports, close to 5% of GDP) but also the flow of ideas and new thinking which are transforming traditional thought patterns across (mostly urban) India.

The Indian diaspora constitute an important global market, with food patterns and cultural habits still, in some manner, tied to their country of origin.

This large **emerging trend of global migration and tribes** has had significant social and business impact both directly as well as indirectly. Joel Kotkin has written a fascinating book on this phenomenon, called, "Tribes".

In direct economic impact we see the emergence of global Indian food brands like "Haldirams", MDH, MTR and Pathak's. Similarly we see Mama Sita, the Filipino food brand, Jollibee the large Filipino burger chain, or Nissin and Marutai noodles from Japan.

Indeed, the "overseas Indian" market has a "GDP" greater than Australia...and companies would do well to take note.

Food habits have also transferred and morphed. We see Pizza, burgers, noodles and Tandoori chicken now become a part of global cuisine. Fusion cuisine is an emerging trend. We see much social media debate on whether pineapples are an acceptable topping on Pizza!

Music and culture is not far behind, as Korean Telenovelas take Asia by storm. The Korean boy band BTS lists annual revenues of US$5 billion, with followers all over the world!

Similarly, overseas Filipinos, Chinese, Mexicans, and others constitute global "tribes" (the authors confess to belong to this tribe of global nomads) that are a fascinating blend of the home and adopted cuisines and cultures.

Their interactions with each other will lead to an emergence of truly global cultures, constituting a growing trend with myriad opportunities.

In their home countries, this helps engender a change of social attitudes and entrenched biases (like regionalism or the caste structure) and leads to increasing awareness of global trends, business, brands, and politics.

Equally, we see also distinct tensions arise as the world globalises and people are concerned that their individuality and unique cultures could be subsumed, thereby leading to several counter-trends towards localisation.

D) The emergence of transnational/multi-ethnic "tribes"

In a similar manner, social media has enabled the evolution of "like-minded" groups that transcend national borders. Whether it is people committed to

"Intermittent Fasting" or "Meditation", or the environment (or, more worryingly, fanaticism of any sort, like the "flat Earthers"), the internet has enabled the creation of "global tribes" who have allegiance to, and find commonality in, shared thoughts, ideals, and ideas.

These loyalties often are stronger than traditional "national" loyalties, and they represent opportunities for enterprise. One well-known example is Manchester United, the global football-loving tribe.

Is the era of the nation-state coming to an end? Certainly, the emergence of economic blocks like the EU or ASEAN point in that direction. This has huge implications for business, as this creates more global groups with common thinking patterns, needs, wants, and perhaps openness to new brand propositions.

2. Institutions of belief systems and religions

Historically, one of the foremost human institutions, organised around collective belief, has been Religion (and associated institutions like the Church/temple/mosque/equivalents or priesthood and equivalents). These created some of the earliest frameworks around which people could organise their behaviours, activities, and economies.

This institution of Religion is also subject to change due to some of the drivers listed previously: the growth of urbanisation, globalisation, new information technology, and emerging ideas of the fragility and interconnectedness of life on this planet.

We will look at this institution along four themes:

A) *Religious institutions that directly support economic activity*

Spirituality remains at the core of most religious institutions, but they traditionally devoted considerable attention to economics, politics, and business.

In medieval times, the Church sponsored new explorations, expansion of trade, and professional guilds. Today, this influence may appear to wane, but the religious institutions remain large, wealthy landowners, like the Catholic Church, for instance, or even the Church of England.

Indeed, with the emergence of concepts such as Islamic Banking (Islam is against the concept of "interest rates", which are classified as usurious or exploitative) or televangelism (several religions), we see continued involvement of religion in business and enterprise.

B) *Religious institutions organising community and governance*

Religion historically created lasting codes of behaviour and cultural "memes" around which societal life could be organised. To do this, they often used promises of rewards and threats of punishment in the "afterlife" if these behaviours were not followed.

Religious institutions also crowned kings, codified laws, and had the power to sanctify marriages and record births, deaths, and succession, thereby ensuring both societal cohesion and continuity of tradition. To some extent, this role continues to be important, though many "secular" people are turning to the state (rather than Religion) to register or solemnise births, weddings, and deaths.

Author's note: A rather sad chapter in the recorded history of organised religions has been the frightening episodes (and justification) of violence against women, against "others" in general, or against those somehow perceived as "less pious", or even in their clashes with each other in their conviction of being the sole owners of "truth".

N.B. In the following sections, we use the word "religion" spelt with a lower-case "r" to distinguish from the earlier, mainstream, accepted "Religions". These new religions have gained fanatical converts across the world and are possibly the fastest-growing global religions based on how they influence and drive new codes of behaviour, creating new cultural "memes".

C) Emerging "religious" institutions of consumerism

In an increasingly secular world, religion takes many forms beyond the traditional ones as individual beliefs are grouped and codified by new institutions, which, in turn, are created by groups of similar-minded people.

Consumerism has effected a great change over the last decades, and Yuval Noah Harari calls this the fastest growing universal religion! Here, he refers to the increasing tendency of consumers around the world to "define" themselves and "identify" with others based on the brands they consume, whether it is the latest Apple device, the car, or handbags.

At the same time, there is a growing evolution of consumer awareness and rights, and the differentiating role of customer delight. Future-thinking organisations like Zappos build their competitive advantage on "customer delight" (as opposed to customer service).

Consumers are also given a voice by social media to air their concerns. They have embraced this voice and often self-organise in an "alliance of the small" to put pressure on or lobby commercial organisations. The movie Erin Brockovich (based on a true story) is an expression of such organisation.

Similarly, small and medium organisations often come together to create buyers' groups or lobby groups to change government policy.

D) Emerging "religious" institutions built around sustainability

Similarly, new "religions" like **sustainability** are emerging. The old Greek concept of "Gaia" is slowly coming back to vogue. As we understand more of the intricacies behind the fine balance that sustains life on Earth, we view our inter-connectedness in broader terms. We discuss more on this in the section that follows.

3. Institutions of enterprise and corporations

A) The "purpose" of business as an institution

The last few centuries have seen the shaping of the global economy and societies by multinational corporations with the primary purpose of enhancing business and profits, much as articulated by noted economist Milton Friedman in his famous piece in the New York Times in 1971, where he thundered, "the purpose of business is business". It was an opinion piece that influenced a generation of business leaders around the world and still resonates with many.

One of the most striking and early examples of a multinational corporation was the East India Company, which colonised India with "Business and Profit" as the only motive. An example that created much misery for the exploited populations of India and still reverberates in the country's deep distrust of multinationals.

Since then, multinationals, particularly in the oil and gas and mining industries, have often been accused of bringing down governments and influencing foreign policy. Some of this criticism is perhaps warranted.

Does the corporation have any purpose beyond profit? Any social responsibility? This is the subject of increasing debate. While there is unlikely to be a definitive answer soon, the very fact that such questions are being raised suggests a new idea is taking hold.

B) Corporations create employment and wealth

Enterprise and multinational corporations have been very successful in mobilising and channelling global capital flows, investment, knowhow transfer, "Best Practice" sharing, and even employment creation (the set-up of low-cost manufacturing locations and BPOs is a case in point) in their search to maximise profits and shareholder wealth creation.

The miracle of the East Asian tiger economies, or even India after "liberalisation" in 1991, all point to the positive effect the corporation can have on reducing poverty and creating wealth in society.

C) Corporations create (access to) public assets (bandwidth, mining rights)

Economic development over the last two centuries has been driven directly by mining of fossil fuels and metals. The resulting ecological impact has, however, created distrust of these corporations.

Today, as "Data becomes the new oil", the large social media giants are being viewed through a similar lens as mining companies.

Large social media companies now have access to data about every facet of their consumers' lives. How this will be used responsibly to enhance services and lives, versus exploiting them solely for profit, will be a key topic of debate as well as regulation going forward.

> Starting in the 90's, the Telecom sector was one of the fastest growing industries globally. People everywhere rushed to buy mobile phones. Governments rushed to auction off "bandwidth", effectively inventing a new sovereign asset. And everywhere the revolution gave rise to new billionaires. (Like Carlos Slim, the Mexican business magnate, and several others all over the world.)
>
> The telecom revolution brought with it a multiplier effect, as people everywhere learnt to incorporate and innovate around this ability to communicate instantly and globally.
>
> Companies like MPesa created **digital payments** systems in Kenya (WeChat and others did the same in China) and the multiplier effect was immediately felt across the economy as more people had access to the formal digital economy.
>
> There is **great potential** for governments to leverage these new sovereign assets to create new industries and bring more people into the formal economy.

Will data also become a national sovereign asset, as China seems to indicate? (All data on Chinese citizens have to be stored within the country, even as Chinese companies are viewed with suspicion for mining data elsewhere to benefit China.)

D) Corporations in a "flatter" world

We see also a trend evolving from the previous three centuries, where brands and companies were largely created in the industrialised North, to one where new, disruptive brands and companies are arising in the South.

This is a good thing, as it diversifies the base from which innovation springs.

And at the same time, we see Western capitalist models being challenged by emerging "State Guided" East Asian models, which often seem to use (in Africa and elsewhere) the playbook of the East India Company to wrest territorial advantage and grab access to raw materials, food, water, and minerals. These are state "owned and guided" transnational corporations, run for the sole benefit of the origin country's global aspirations and strategy.

Critics argue that the generous initial terms by China disguise a longer-term plan to grab territory and access to water and minerals, much in the manner of the East India company two centuries earlier. Indeed, the 100-year lease on Hambantota port in Sri Lanka seems to indicate this view is not without merit.

E) Corporate governance will shape the evolution of this institution

In recent times, the emergence of the "ESG" (Environmental, Social, and Governance) challenge has been an important new area for corporates to look at.

• *We have already looked at "sustainability" in the context of religion*

There is the indisputable fact that, as the human population grows from the current 7 billion to peak at 10 billion by mid-century, the planet needs to provide

50% more food and 50% more energy at a minimum, compared to current levels. And far greater, if one accounts for growing aspirations of societies to consume at the levels of American or European societies.

There is a growing realisation that this demand, while understandable and justifiable from human societies' point of view, exceeds the carrying capacity of the planet, and therefore, we need to reinvent lifestyles, concepts of social and economic equity, and business models.

There is increasing focus on enterprise solutions for sustainability, driven by the **"3R's"** thinking. **"Reduce, Reuse, Recycle".**

How to move from "use and throw away" business models to circular business models. The World Economic Forum has argued that this may be the largest new business opportunity ever seen by mankind.

So there is increasing focus on "product as a service" business models. (For years Rolls Royce did not sell aircraft engines, but sold "operating hours" and took charge of engine maintenance themselves.)

Imagine as a thought experiment, if that concept were to go mainstream. You would not any more buy that refrigerator, car, smart phone. You would buy instead the "time of use" and the company would take charge of maintenance, recycle, reuse. Creating convenience for the user, and recurring revenue steams for themselves, while saving the environment.

A win-win business model.

Shareholder activism has also seen an increase. Castrol recently saw the example where activists voted sustainability advocates into the board!! Microsoft saw shareholder action to ensure better protection against gender based harassment.

Carbon trading mechanisms are also growing and creating new economic opportunities for enterprise.

To be fair, there remain challenges from several developing economies, who point to the excessive use of resources per capita in the industrialised north. And seek leeway to continue potentially environmentally hazardous practices a while longer. Or to get subsidised for adopting new technologies.

The overall trend, however, is unmistakeable.

There is greater understanding of the frightening evolution of the ecosphere, resulting in potentially irreversible Climate Change and the largest man-made mass extinction of species of life.

Given the failure of governments and traditional institutions in ensuring a sustainable ecology, people are holding big business accountable. New institutions are emerging, like Greenpeace or shareholder activist groups that directly pressure corporations to change their behaviours.

The opportunities created by business in response to this challenge will define the successful companies of the coming century.

• *There is a growing understanding of the importance of diversity*

Companies today embrace a global workforce and try to tap into the creative energies of all their people, irrespective of gender or race. In parallel, social mores have evolved with acceptance of alternate sexual orientations. Acceptance for "LGBTQ" is increasingly becoming a "litmus" test through which Millennials and liberals view countries and corporations.

• *Governance models*

With access to data, far greater transparency exists. How do you make, execute, and communicate decisions – especially when there is nothing private anymore?

We're moving from the monolithic organisation that catered to all parts of the value chain to an emerging model, where there are ecosystems of business partners across the value chain.

This unbundling of traditionally successful organisational models and emerging disruptive models will create new business opportunities.

4. Institutions of governance – national, international, and political/economic/corporate

It is useful to look at Generation Z, or Millennials' view on employment, motivation and loyalty. As has been argued convincingly in his much watched video on YouTube, Simon Sinek notes that this generation is not motivated by dreams of money or material symbols of success, as their parents were.

Instead, they look for **purpose.** (purpose of a corporation, and it's brands). They look at how the company behaves on issues that matter to them.

Sustainability. Diversity and Inclusion. Respect for communities and attitudes. Data access. Nothing is "internal and confidential" any more.

And if they don't find what they seek, they create a startup that resonates with these values.

Note the star athlete from the US, and woman to win the most Olympic medals ever. Allyson Felix was sidelined as an endorser by Nike when she got pregnant. She launched her own brand of footwear (Saysh), and came back stronger than ever in the 2021 Tokyo Olympics to bring her total medal tally to 11.

A) The role of local government in shaping economies and corporations

Roles and responsibilities of governments have evolved through the ages, as we shifted from tribal societies to monarchies and thereafter to newer systems of democracy, autocracy, or socialism/communism.

To start with, governments saw themselves as custodians of their citizens fundamental rights and duties. They provided much-needed safety and security, regulated economic activity, and guaranteed property rights.

And in the process, they abrogated to themselves the power to tax, to punish, and to reward and regulate people's lives and behaviours, increasingly taking away authority from the family, the Church, and from local communities.

As far as country governance models go, pendulums everywhere are swinging strangely between capitalism and socialism. China is now the centre of global capitalism, though with a "state guided" face. The largest emerging global multinationals are Chinese owned and guided. At the same time, Europe, which was so capitalist-oriented over the last few centuries, is emerging as the global capital of socialism, with universal health care and concepts, such as "Universal Basic Income" being debated.

Expectations from government are changing everywhere, though. Both citizens and enterprise now look to government to create conditions for economic growth. Above all, business looks for predictability in the economic environment so that they can minimise the risks inherent in new investments.

This calls for predictability in laws and taxation, and economic incentives to attract investment that creates infrastructure and jobs. Governments everywhere now compete to create conditions to attract business. For enterprise, this is a welcome evolution in this institution!

B) Institutions of global governance

Over the last two centuries, we saw global systems and institutions like the IMF, the UN, the World Bank, and the G8 dominated by countries and economies from the "North", often dictating policies to weaker nations.

As economic pendulums shift (discussed in an earlier chapter), the composition of these institutions itself is changing to accommodate China, India, Brazil, and others.

With economic clout growing, China has pioneered the "Belt and Road initiative" for trade and economic development. And the Asia infrastructure investment bank, funded jointly by China and India.

We see "South-South" capital flows becoming ever more important and replacing "North- South" capital flows as the major component of global capital flows. The emerging "ASEAN +6" common market and economic zone, if it comes into reality, promises to be the single largest economic block and economic engine on the planet.

Of course, this has implications for governance and monitoring cross border economic activity, including corruption. It is interesting to note that the BRICS countries share notes on corruption and cross-fertilise methods to control it.

C) Creating transparency to support a level playing field

We see the enactment of the "Right to Information" bill in India as indicative of the changes enabled by digital means in ensuring good governance. Today, any concerned citizen can seek to access the status of his file or his request and read all the comments therein.

D) Public-private partnerships as an emerging institution to nurture growth

New models of enterprise are evolving, where public institutions collaborate with private and commercial enterprise to create innovative models for public good, such as building roads and expressways or high-speed train lines or even laying fibre optic cable. This is an interesting development which promises to open up new avenues of growth for enterprise.

An interesting example of the **evolution of governance** has been the **use of technology in India.** The **"Aadhar"** card in India has linked 130 billion citizens to the digital economy. It stores data on each citizen, including biomarkers, is linked to bank accounts, mobile phones, and health insurance.

This enables the elimination of middlemen, and enables efficient direct bank transfers. As a result, corruption (which earlier corroded institutions and governance) has reduced significantly.

A striking example is the nationwide elections conducted in India once every five years, where the largest electorate on the planet votes democratically, safely, without fraud. And the results are collated digitally within days.

E) The political economy and related institutions of feudalism and other "isms"

The weakening of the feudal system (see box) and increased freedom, in turn, created more opportunities for economies and business. After 1600 AD, the growth of democratic institutions, combined with the Industrial Revolution, shifted the focus of wealth creation to capital.

Traditionally, economists defined an economy as being driven by four factors: **land, labour, capital, and enterprise.** From the earliest civilisations, leading up to about 1600 AD, the economy was primarily driven by land and labour.

How wealthy one was, depended on how much land one had, and how many people one had to work the land. Simply put, the fastest way to get wealthy was to invade one's neighbour, seize his land, and enslave him to work on his (erstwhile) land.

Most political institutions and systems were feudal, and sadly, slavery was a key component of traditional economies.

This institution was demolished by the French Revolution, the American Civil War, and various struggles for independence across the former colonial world.

The Industrial Revolution meant that the fastest way to create wealth was to deploy capital to invest in factories that broke down manufacturing into simpler, repeatable tasks which could be automated with machines, and that thereby created more production, leading to greater wealth.

In the early days of the Industrial Revolution, capital was not easy to access, however, and this led to the tremendous growth of modern banking systems, fuelling unprecedented global expansion and a growth in prosperity.

As a result of this sustained economic boom, today, most

Class, caste, and racial barriers do remain in place in many societies, but are hopefully weakening over time in any urban society that has decisively embraced **the new "talent led" economy.**

Activism, awareness, and regulatory frameworks do also help in eradicating these obstacles to inclusiveness and growth.

To be fair, there are retrograde societies in Syria, Afghanistan, Pakistan, Venezuela, and North Korea (to name a few) where the feudal system appears to grow ever stronger, and there is a yearning to return to the violent, feudal, "predictable" past.

Time will tell what implications this has for them, their neighbours, and for business and enterprise that increasingly is built on creativity, freedom of expression, and intellectual property.

Even in India, caste remains a strong influence in marriages and social interactions, particularly in rural areas. In urban areas, we do see a gradual weakening of its pervasiveness along with political focus on affirmative action.

middle-class people can enjoy a lifestyle similar to Louis IV: wear what they like, go where they like, in the style they choose. Eat what they like and when (ref.: Matt Ridley, "The Rational Optimist").

Today however, the world is awash in capital, looking for opportunities and ideas to invest in. With the "flattening of the world" (ref.: Thomas Friedman), driven by tech, the future now belongs once again to *Labour*, but in a different sense from the Middle Ages.

Now, it is **people** who will creatively apply tech to resolve societal and environmental problems in new ways, learning from natural processes and then mimicking them.

F) Emerging institutions of enterprise

Witness the phenomenal success of Silicon Valley, where a confluence of human talent, venture capital, universities, and academia, combined with a supportive government, has led to the biggest wealth-creation engine ever seen.

No wonder governments all over the world now seek to copy the Silicon Valley model. It is by now well understood that **intellectual capital** will invent the disruptive models and processes which will create the new wealth of the 21st century. Capital is therefore drawn irresistibly to great ideas and to creative people. **Intellectual property creation** is the new game in town.

This is typified by the venture capital industry, which is in search of great founder teams and ideas to invest in, all over the world.

Of course, for every new project that succeeds there are several dozen which fail, and the skill of the VC is as much in

> The venture capital industry has been central to the growth of the new economy. The world is awash in capital, looking for profitable growth opportunities to invest in.
>
> Not surprisingly, some of this has found its way to startups enabled by technology that seek to re-create traditional value chains and offer new value to consumers. Almost every family office, high net worth individual and large corporate is flirting with this. Often with little experience, as they seek to "learn on the job". What makes it especially risky is that over 90% of startups fail and the investors lose their capital.
>
> **Today, India is one of the hottest new destinations for venture capital, apart from the US, Israel, and China.**

selecting the right people to back as it is in having a portfolio of startups where a few big wins will compensate (and more) for those that fail.

To misquote Peter Drucker, the future belongs to societies that create the right conditions for implementing the "vision of Karl Marx, enabled with the power of Bill Gates". Societies that prepare for the future will focus on empowering and training their people, liberating their creativity, and helping provide access to global opportunities.

5. Other institutions shaping life spaces
(a case study of education to illustrate the unbundling of institutions)

Institutions in important life-spaces, like health care, justice, and education, significantly shape human life and society. There are massive disruptions happening in each one of these, driven by technology and changing societal needs; often, with a spill-over throwing up opportunities for enterprise. This section illustrates these disruptions with the help of one such case study in "Education" which is being unbundled to create huge new business opportunities.

Traditionally, education was responsible for the following five activities and created value by bringing them all under one roof:

*   **Knowledge creation**

*   **Knowledge dissemination**

*   **Certification**

*   **Job matching**

*   **Networking**

With improving technology, however, we see these being unbundled and emerging as distinct opportunities for value creation in the education service sector.

Knowledge creation is no longer the preserve of universities. Think tanks, consulting organisations, and even media are commissioning research and churning out new knowledge.

A quick search on Google reveals the interesting factoid: Buckminster Fuller created the "knowledge doubling curve" by estimating that human knowledge doubled each century up to the year 1900. Since

> **IMPLICATIONS OF THIS 'UNBUNDLING' FOR ENTERPRISE.**
>
> Today we see the emergence of several digital education and certification models. Coursera, Edex, BYJU'S, Udacity, Eruditis, to mention just a few.
>
> Some like BYJU'S are already valued in the "Billions", and there are new startups emerging every month in search of the next big growth opportunity.
>
> Such exponential growth inevitably brings allegations of misdoings and lax standards. In response, China has initiated a crackdown on Ed Tech in an attempt to regulate it.

then, this accelerated, and by the Second World War, it was apparently doubling every 25 years. Today, it might be doubling as quickly as every year, and IBM reportedly estimates that the "internet of things" will lead to knowledge doubling every 12 hours!!

Knowledge dissemination models have been challenged with the rise of the Khan Academy, Coursera, EdEx, BYJU'S, and a multitude of digital offerings. No wonder traditional universities are finding it difficult to survive.

The late Harvard Business School Professor Clayton Christiansen predicted (Forbes, Dec. 13, 2018) that half of colleges and universities would close or go bankrupt in the next decade.

This creates huge opportunities for private enterprise because of the sheer scale of demand. Tech-related disruption will mean continuous, lifelong learning will be key to employment.

Lifelong education will be the single-largest, emerging disruptive business opportunity over the next decade.

In a similar vein, new companies are setting up to offer **certification** programs. LinkedIn and others are implementing **job search** and **networking** services. Several other job search portals are already hugely successful, including Monster, Naukri.com, and others.

Is the future starting to look like the distant past, with lifelong learning (and working) systems being the norm?

— — — — — — — — —

As we see, powerful forces of change are coalescing to re-shape our social institutions, unbundling and recreating them.

Our social institutions are the guideposts that shape the behaviour of individuals and organisations alike. Understanding how these institutions are transforming, with changes rippling through into our life spaces and society, is key to understand the future of enterprise.

Part II

How We Do

How Technologies Power Disruption and Re-imagine Our World

Disruption in the way we do things has powered pivotal shifts of history. The shift to agriculture. Or even the Industrial Revolution.

Today we see, once again, technology driving a revolution and bringing about a fundamental restructuring of our society, the way we think, define ourselves, live, work, and play. Reshaping industry and enterprise.

We stand on the brink of an unprecedented technological revolution.

*A surge of digital technologies is radically transforming our world into one founded on a "**connected, digital, intelligent**" reality that is fundamentally different from the physically defined world of the past.*

This transformational change is founded on the confluence of **three powerful streams** of technologically enabled ideas:

- **The first, an intense, ubiquitous connectivity, so our world connects moments, people, actions, our thoughts, and desires at the speed of light.**

- **A world now migrating to an increasingly tangible and vivid metaverse of digital identities and interactions.**

- **Distributed intelligence that pervades this metaverse magnifies changes and is seamlessly available, 24/7. To power every thought and every action.**

Each stream merges with the others and creates a tsunami of changes, the outlines of which we can barely begin to imagine.

Digital tech is not merely introducing change. It is re-imagining our world in every possible way – be it the way we live, work, or play. Indeed, every domain of human endeavour.

Breakthroughs are happening every day in domains as diverse as medicine, mathematics, and materials. Waves of new discoveries that promise continued disruptions over time.

In the subsequent chapters, we look at the technological transformations which are the foundation for changes in every domain of work and life. And the epochal opportunities that are opening to those who are willing to seize them.

DOI: 10.4324/9781003254737-8

Chapter 7

Ubiquitous Connectivity

The Foundation of an Anytime, Anywhere World

The advances of social media, driverless cars, cashless payments, work from home, or even OTT entertainment: these are just a few examples of how disruptive digital technologies are radically transforming our world.

*Connectivity is **the very foundation of this new, re-imagined** world that is emerging. Technology extends our reach into every moment, every place, and to everyone (or thing!). Seamless action across boundaries powers changes in the way we live, play, work, and interact.*

*Today, connectivity is not only becoming even more powerful but is expanding to new dimensions, transforming, to become a **ubiquitous connectivity**, enabling thereby a universe of possibilities.*

It all started with a phone. A phone that happened to be mobile.

And today connectivity is becoming the **very foundation** for a **new, re-imagined** world.

In this chapter, we look at connectivity, its impact,

> ### THE ORIGIN: IT ALL STARTED WITH A PHONE THAT HAPPENED TO BE MOBILE
>
> The first demo of mobile technology was in 1973 by Motorola with a phone that weighed 2 kilos. And 1983 saw the first handheld mobile phone, the Motorola DynaTAC8000X at a price of $4000!
>
> The technology started taking off in the 1990s with the introduction of 2G and digital technologies. **And the world started to change.**

insights, and implications. What is the scale of its impact? What is the deep human energy unleashed by it? What are the technological advances that are transforming the notion of connectivity, and in turn, transforming our lives?

I. CONNECTIVITY BECOMES A UNIVERSAL ENGINE FOR MODERN LIFE

People have embraced connectivity in record numbers and at record speed. Never before in human history has there been such a swift and radical explosion of any new technology. Over 8 billion people use mobiles, over 65% of the population, and perhaps more than any single product category.

People perceive enormous value in connectivity.

DOI: 10.4324/9781003254737-9

Consumers see the value in everyday life and communication, professionally as well as socially. However, mobiles seem especially important for emerging-market consumers. According to a BCG study[1], "in China and India, the consumer-reported benefits from mobile phones could exceed 40 percent of average income".

Businesses feel the difference – SMEs that are mobile leaders "use mobile services more intensively, see their revenues growing up to two times faster and add jobs up to eight times faster than their peers who are laggards".

New businesses anchored on connectivity are disrupting and creating new markets.

The industry has burgeoned. Mainstream mobile technologies drive the world economy generating over $1 trillion in annual revenues today and growing at twice the rate of GDP growth.

Unprecedented value is being created – 6 of the 25 most valuable companies in the world are participants in the mobile value chain – Apple, Google, China Mobile, Alibaba, Facebook (Meta), and Verizon. Many of the world's richest people have multiplied their fortunes with telecom.

Connectivity is becoming the foundation of our lives and enterprise.

The value of this industry, large as it is, is relatively small, compared to the transformation it has triggered (just like previous centuries discovered that the value added by railroads was exponentially greater than the revenues of the railroad business).

The mobile phone has changed human life more than anything else. It is our most treasured possession. Its enormous value has rapidly driven an almost universal adoption.

Large new industries have emerged that ride on connectivity. E-commerce, digital transactions, social media, and even new innovations on the horizon like autonomous transport. Powerful new interventions include the public health management in the Covid crisis and governance initiatives like the Aadhar identity program for over 1 billion Indians. Connectivity's importance is widespread and critical to our emerging world – the economy, human lives, business, health, governance, and into every field of endeavour.

And note the startling rapidity of transformation – a lot of this change has gathered steam in just the last decade!

2. THE TRANSFORMATION(S) OF CONNECTIVITY. TRANSFORMATION BY CONNECTIVITY

How could something as simple as a mobile phone make such an impact? An impact that is huge, and yet just starting to build up.

The truth is that, in just a little over a decade, the concept of connectivity has morphed radically. From its origin as merely a phone, albeit with a valuable mobility feature, it has been transformed by **five big themes**.[2] These technological developments have not merely strengthened connectivity but have added **valuable new dimensions** to it.

A) Functionality multiplied with handiness and connectivity

The mobile phone has absorbed different applications with a steady stream of innovations. Messaging was the first add-on to the voice of phones, absorbing the "pager" and rendering it obsolete.

The next big step was facilitated by the built-in camera. Not just a combo device, it added great relevance with its handiness to capture many more moments. Cameras went out of fashion.

Pictures were transformed from the posed to the spontaneous and the useful. And what's more, the pictures could be shared! Life and behaviours changed.

This was a landmark, signalling innovations that would change industries seemingly disconnected from mobile phones. Consumer lives soon had more pictures but no cameras; time checks but no watches! Better cameras, video, and special effects followed and still are driving growth. In quick succession, music, health monitoring, PDAs, and many more functionalities are integrating with the mobile.

A transformation journey from a phone that happened to be mobile to a mobile that has a phone.

B) The app is it! The software multiplier

If our lives today revolve around the mobile phones, then apps are the very centre point!

Today, with over a $100 billion dollar in sales, an enormous width of applications can be seen. Indeed, it is difficult to believe that the first app only appeared in 2007 with the launch of the iPhone.

A closer look at the app phenomenon provides valuable insights on their powerful impact on everyday life and their potential for future opportunities.

Apps started as small add-ons to provide functionalities for mobile phones (e.g., the clock app or the daily planner) – handy tools which added value. Next, companies created stand-alone apps, independent product offerings, often purely digital apps, like Tik Tok, gaming apps, and fitness tools. An exponentially increasing list that today extends to virtually every domain. These innovations are creating powerful revenue streams. Many of these have a global appeal and are ramping up to be amongst the most valuable businesses worldwide.

> ### THE OPPORTUNITY OF APPS
>
> "In 2020, mobile app consumer spending on the Google Play and Apple App Store amounted to 102 billion U.S. dollars worldwide. The two app market leaders reported a combined 142 million app downloads that year, with social media, gaming, and messaging apps accounting for the largest share of downloads."
>
> (Mobile internet usage worldwide - statistics & facts | Statista)

In parallel, apps have become the way for existing businesses to engage with their customers, provide services, and drive purchase.

• What drives the success of apps

Benefits connect to the moment

Apps funnel in an invaluable functionality to users whenever needed.

Access your bank, see the map when you are lost, or even window shop from the convenience of your armchair.

Having the benefit at the "now" moment is enticing and transforms how consumers seek benefits. For everything. We see apps transforming fitness and health, governance, education, ordering a cab, shopping, banking, and connecting with WhatsApp, email, or that Facebook update. An app opportunity exists everywhere.

The customer is at the heart of it

Apps connect to an individual and their need of the moment. They help fulfil the long-standing business promise of making the customer Queen (or King), addressing their specific need. Successful apps, are not merely sites available on a phone, they are focussed on customer "application" and score significantly better than any website. Apps add significant commercial and relationship value. According to recent study reported in Marketing.com.au, "In-app purchases are 130% higher than on the mobile web. We know that consumers view more products per session and have a higher 'add-to-cart' rate on apps compared to websites."

• The business implication of apps

For entrepreneurs and innovators, apps open up new markets and enable new creative tools and access to customers. Apps with their own marketplaces help build new businesses.

Apps are surging ahead; worldwide downloads grew by 25% in the first half of 2020. But one statistic showcases the power of connectedness and apps: according to a study published in zdnet.com, "consumers spent 1.6 trillion hours on mobile in the first half of 2020" with over 4.3 hours per day on apps. As is evident, an intense connection to consumers exists.

Integrating new technologies in computation, sensors, and connectivity (e.g., 5G, better augmented reality) can add enormous value to the connectedness (e.g., richer virtual buying experiences).

C) The advent of smart phones: the leap of connected computation

In the 1990s, at a time when computers and laptops were surging and mobiles were largely phones, a revolutionary possibility was glimpsed: "Perhaps phones could replace computers as the device of the future?"

Indeed, increased computation and storage power makes today's smart phones, iPhones, or similar versions of Android phones as powerful as most computers. But what makes them invaluable is in the way they can assist us with their handiness and the ability to connect computational value into the moment people need it most.

Smart phones moved computation power beyond corporates to individual usage, transformed from merely servicing business applications to changing lives of the man on the street. Unshackled from desktops, they impacted the need of the place and the moment. Bill Gates and Paul Allen's vision of "a computer at every desk" had morphed into "one in every hand"!

A totally new world of opportunities has emerged. Computational-based consumer businesses opportunities today are valued in the trillions of dollars. This will grow exponentially with the explosion in smart phone penetration and the increase in consumer adoption of such services.

For telecom companies, this fuels the mega-shift from "voice" to "data". The revenue value of data services is expected to form the majority of revenues for mobile telephony companies. A shift which is getting increasing momentum with a progressive evolution to more digitally savvy consumers and the emergence of high-relevance applications.

The value to consumers is even greater – truly priceless. Connected computation is not just the foundation of apps but has enabled the entire power of the metaverse – our digital world that moves with us.

Mobiles have morphed from being telephony to becoming a platform for life.

• Connecting everyone: democratisation of the digital revolution

The costs of mobiles – and connectivity – is dropping, even as their features and powers are exploding. Connectivity, computation, and their benefits can potentially be universal.

This leads to several big opportunities:

— It opens the doors for the full power of the digital revolution to benefit the common man as, for example, applications like discovery of produce prices for marginal farmers. Nandan Nilekani insightfully observes that data in the developing world is not a tool to be used by the rich but an essential to getting rich.

— Universal adoption of smart phones is providing primary access to the internet. And with increasing digital savviness of consumers, this is becoming a key commercial tool to widen the business footprint. Companies like Flipkart (a Walmart-acquired e-commerce player) has used an app-only business model to reach hinterland India.

— Government programs often have a need to reach everyone. And universal connectivity enables superior delivery of applications facilitating development and governance. During the Covid crisis, the power of connectivity drove invaluable social awareness and action, impacting the well-being of billions. Increasingly, connectivity is transforming government action, enabling many services and messages to be delivered directly into the phone of every citizen.

— Identity platforms using phone-based digital identities are simplifying banking and other verifications. As connectivity reaches everyone, our mobile connection becomes our identity.

• The power of networks: new benefits plus disruptive new connections

Connectivity (using apps and diverse technologies) builds networks. And networks can generate **new benefits,** changing life and businesses alike; social networking is a powerful example.

— Apps build a **connected set of customers**. This linked network of customers is a valuable re-marketing avenue and is becoming the most valuable asset for businesses. It is increasingly monetised not just with product extensions but by creating "super apps" cutting across multiple verticals. Companies like Tencent have harnessed their customer network to build an empire of financial services, becoming, in the process, one of the most valuable companies in the world.

— Networks and digital processes have been improving business effectiveness for decades but largely focussed on internal processes' efficiencies. With mobile phones, today, businesses have been connected to the heart of consumer action; every business function can draw upon and respond to the consumer, often in real time. Superior connected solutions – OTT, for example – add value to the re-imagined life of consumers seeking benefits . in the moment.

Apps leverage consumer connectivity, facilitating processes like customer acquisition and fulfilment. Even business analytics has a heightened customer focus, making micro-marketing and even supply chains more effective. Consumers have been pivoted to the centre of businesses. A **new consumer-centricity** is transforming business processes and unleashing new possibilities.

— One of the most significant outcomes of connectivity is the ability to form **platforms that connect different sets** of people – buyers and sellers, advertisers and consumers, or even other stakeholders (like banks financing purchases online). Getting people, products, and data together: this is creating entirely new ways for markets to operate. Reducing barriers to entry, building new efficiencies, and introducing disruptive benefits (like network-based optimisation in car hailing apps). It is the foundation for some of the most salient businesses of today: Amazon (and many marketplaces), LinkedIn, Air BnB, Facebook (Meta), Uber, and Google. Imaginative use of platforms and technologies is providing new business models with a potential to transform almost every sector.

3. TECHNOLOGY ADVANCES ARE MAKING CONNECTIVITY UBIQUITOUS AND POWERFUL

Breakthrough technologies are enhancing the power to connect. Reaching out to more people and places, with more power of connection, with more ease. Three big themes are driving this transformation. As we explore them, we will uncover innovation streams that show promise to make never-before benefits possible. Each can fundamentally change the way we live, and each creates enormous economic value.

> ### 5G - THE NEW OPPORTUNITY
>
> 1) The new superhighway for the **digital world-** Dramatically higher speeds. Greater data capacity. Ultra-low latency.
>
> 2) A new world of benefits e.g. self-driving cars, enabling **IoT** with billions of connections, hi-speed graphic applications.
>
> 3) Very high front ended investments. In advance of widespread adoption.
>
> 4) An opportunity for businesses and technologies building an **ecosystem** spanning telecom infrastructure, networks, and software which stitches it together. And for creation of powerful new platforms and middleware. For the entire world!

A) More powerful and versatile connectivity

The archetypal tech is 5G, which comes off a string of generations (2G, 3G, 4G) of telecom technologies that have introduced quantum shifts over time. 5G delivers heightened speed, greater capacity, and ultra-low latency.

The simple, two-letter acronym hides the size of the opportunity and also the complexity of the change. Formerly unimaginable opportunities, like self-driving cars, now promise to be a reality. A whole ecosystem of valuable businesses is generated (see graphic). The future highway of the digital world is created, serving as the infrastructure of connectivity. But this comes with its own challenges. The changeover to 5G worldwide is an investment comparable to building our entire highway system anew in a short period of time.

There are a host of other technologies; Deloitte lists the following: "low Earth orbit satellites, mesh networks, edge computing, and ultra-broadband solutions. These promise order-of-magnitude improvements that will support reliable, high-performance communication capabilities; software-defined networking and network functions".

Networking can drive digital transformation as well as enable networking-dependent technologies like IoT, block chain, and advanced analytics with their respective disruptive impacts.

In parallel, connectivity is becoming more ubiquitous, with Wi-Fi and near-field technologies driving universal adoption and 24/7 access, everywhere.

B) Seamless connection

A different set of technologies is improving the human connection. Advances in translation are breaking language barriers. Handwriting digitisation technologies make even prescriptions intelligible. Virtual personal assistants with voice and image inputs seamlessly connect the human world with the digital universe. Perhaps even more significant, cloud technologies can potentially link the individual to almost unlimited knowledge and processing capabilities.

In the foreseeable future, inputs will no longer have to be "entered"; communication will be frictionless and dumb interfaces will be replaced by speech-based ones. Vanishing barriers have enormous transformative potential, enhancing the use of connectivity across a wide set of everyday human applications.

> **THE POWER OF SEAMLESSNESS**
>
> **"Babel Fish from The Hitchhiker's Guide to the Galaxy,"** (science fiction novel). The Babel Fish was a small, bright yellow fish. If you put it in your ear, it would feed off brainwaves around you and let you understand anyone who spoke to you,"
>
> "Perhaps wireless earbuds translate voices and smart glasses that translate text could transform the tourism industry, giving people more confidence to travel/live in countries where they don't know the native language. Improvements in machine learning, smart wearable devices, and augmented reality could enable other helpful features.

C) Connectivity to every thing

Over time, mobiles have changed lifestyles, adding devices like cameras to our connection. A new dimension of connectivity is being enabled by The Internet of Things (IoT), which refers to a network of connected "smart" devices that are linked via the internet and communicate seamlessly.

Along with advances in sensors, this extension of connectivity to machines is enabling automation of actions in remote places, continually, across time. Real-time data, tracking soil moisture and nutrients, can be transmitted wirelessly to agricultural experts for advice and assistance.

Similarly, security and alarm systems (like Amazon Ring, for example), equipped with long-life batteries, or electricity connections, provide homeowners with the peace of mind to keep track of one's house or even elders living alone. IoT shows the promise to underpin a new "smart" world of beings and things!

In recent years, fitness devices like Fitbit and the Apple Watch, which track activity levels and provide real-time data on heart rate and other health indicators, have seen widespread adoption. Similarly, trackers for pets. All these devices and applications share one common characteristic: dependence on strong and uninterrupted connectivity.

"In the future, it is likely that the smart phone will not be separated from you at all. It may be embedded in your body or brain, constantly scanning your biometric data and your emotions", writes Yuval Noah Harari in "The Rise of Connectivity – Information Services & Technology Ungated".

IoT connections already outnumber mobile phone connections. With the advent of 5G and the growth of popular applications, this is number is likely to grow manifold, outdoing even the explosive growth of mobiles; semiconductors will be everywhere. Wearable technology will take this ubiquity even further.

The sum of these connectivity advances could blur the lines of reality as we know it and take seamlessness to a new dimension.

4. THE POWER BEHIND CONNECTIVITY: UNLEASHING THE POWER OF THE MOMENT

> Mobile phones initiated the surge of connectivity. But a much more powerful concept than mere telephony drives its disruptive impact. Consumer connectivity is unlocking the power of the moment. It enables the individual to **connect the moment** with a world of resources needed at the moment. Seamlessly and powerfully.
>
> Connectivity is **enabling powerful action** at the moment. Actions that go far beyond having a voice conversation, or even using a handy camera device on the phone. It connects to driving virtually any action across boundaries: to do a money transfer to a bank, to order food, or to entertain. From pre-planned action to pulling the solution for the need of the moment, connectivity becomes an agile construct. It can entail not just physical actions but ideas, information, learning, anything to help make more of the moment, with enormous speed and flexibility.
>
> Connectivity is indeed about unlocking the power of the moment -whenever, wherever and for whatever. Everyday emerging new technologies are enhancing its disruptive impact. We are truly moving to "an anytime, anywhere" world whose foundation is connected.

The **power of connectivity** is being exponentially enhanced by two equally disruptive streams of change:

- **The digital metaverse**, which is developing into virtually a parallel new world for individuals and organisations alike. A world you can connect to and act for every possible task or facet of life. Whether to gossip, shop, educate, or whatever. If mobiles introduced the powerful ability to connect, then the **metaverse adds purpose and value to the connectivity**.

- **Addition of intelligence dramatically adds power to the action**. Advancements in computation, analytics, and AI enable human-like intelligence to be added to tasks, enhancing benefits delivered by connecting to the metaverse.

As these three streams synergise to add value, every aspect of our lives is getting re-imagined: the way we work, play, and live; perhaps even the very essence of human purpose.

In subsequent chapters, we take a closer look at the emerging metaverse and disruption by the addition of intelligence.

NOTE

1 https://www.bcg.com/publications/2015/telecommunications-technology-industries-the-mobile-revolution.
2 In this part, successive chapters focus on the big technology streams to understand them and draw out their disruptive potential. In part III, we draw upon these powerful themes as we seek routes to seize the change opportunity.

Chapter 8

Life and Identity in the Metaverse

The Internet Revolution – Platform for a New World

The internet is the technology that will shape the Information Age, much as electricity helped shape the Industrial Age. As we enter this "information age", we see a fundamental re-shaping of the industrial and social revolutions that characterised the last 100 years.

We see, all over the world, societies, identities, and social interactions being re-shaped by the hyper-connectivity and social platforms unleashed. . . . The internet and the new metaverse promise to transform how we work, how we play, how we keep ourselves entertained, connect socially; indeed, even how we define ourselves.

And how we live life.

This is probably the most fundamental transformation. A shift in the space in which we "live" and "experience life". From the 3D "real" world into the "metaverse".

One that seamlessly blends our "physical reality" with "virtual reality" spaces in which we interact for work (with work from home gaining currency) and interact socially.

This transformation can be explored along six dimensions in its impact.

And we shall see in this chapter that each dimension opens tremendous opportunities for enterprise.

1. **The scale of this change, the speed, and the ubiquity**

2. **The evolution of a distinct digital social identity that shapes how we interact and with whom**

3. **The resulting impact on how we interact with markets and marketplaces**

4. **Impact on commerce and transactions**

5. **Impact on education**

6. **Impact on governance**

DOI: 10.4324/9781003254737-10

I. THE ORIGINS: UNDERSTANDING THE SCALE OF THIS CHANGE, THE SPEED, THE UBIQUITY, AND THE TRANSFORMATION

THE INTERNET IS UBIQUITOUS IN OUR LIVES.

Poor farmers use it to check commodity prices even as they decide to take their produce to the market. They haven't yet learned to use this tool to completely eliminate the middleman trader/buyer/financier, but with farm law reforms, that day can't be too far away.

Shubham Jaglan, the ten-year-old prodigy from the state of Haryana in India, the son of a milkman, reportedly (media reports) learnt how to play golf by watching YouTube videos. In 2015, he won in the nine-to-ten age category, the IMG Academy junior world golf championship!

Mathematics tutors in Bangalore use the internet to teach kids around the world and check their homework. The internet has a profound and transformative effect

Starting with an estimated 40 million global users in 1996, the internet has grown rapidly to reach almost 5 billion people with internet access today. This speed is mirrored only by the speed of wireless access, which has moved from around 16 million subscribers in 1991 to (as of 2017) over 7 billion subscribers worldwide . . . covering almost the entire human population!

This speed is particularly impressive if one notes that, as of date, unfettered electricity access from the Industrial Revolution 2.0 has still not reached this scale; several villages across South Asia and Africa are still without access to electricity!

The initial application of internet technology was mostly for email communications.

The year 2004 was a landmark. That year, Myspace became the first social media site to reach the milestone of a million monthly active users. And Facebook started in Feb. 2004 in Cambridge, Massachusetts. This is arguably the beginning of social media as we know it.

The social media revolution ushered in by Facebook, LinkedIn, Instagram, Twitter, and their counterparts, each with distinct patterns of interaction and digital identity (see next section), have led to profound changes, at scale,[1] in our very identity . . . a change whose impact and enormity we are only beginning to understand today.

We have moved to an era where we live part of our lives and define our identities in the digital world. (Statista.com estimates the average time users spend on social media per day, worldwide, is 145 minutes!)

And as we "live" and interact digitally, our **life-spaces** are moving with us. Media and advertising seeking a connect were the first to move and, in quick succession, our market places, our commercial interactions. Our life-spaces and institutions of education, health, governance, work, and play – every aspect of life – soon found a powerful relevance in the digital connection.

We increasingly "reside" and conduct our lives and business in **a metaverse, a parallel virtual world,** where people and institutions/organisations exist – their identities, abilities, and interactions powering life. Every day, developments are making this world more significant, all-encompassing, and "real".[2]

We are seeing this digital world, enabled by ubiquitous connectivity and multiplied by intelligence, ripple at warp speed through all facets of life, re-imagining society, lives, life-spaces, and institutions; transforming all levels of society, irrespective of socio-economic status or national boundaries.

2. THE EVOLUTION OF A DISTINCT DIGITAL SOCIAL IDENTITY THAT SHAPES HOW WE INTERACT AND WITH WHOM

At one level, this is essentially **a shift of identity** . . . the creation of new digital "persona".

Adding to this involvement with the virtual world is the invention of "virtual avatars" which reflect how we wish to be perceived in this new, immersive reality we are starting to create. We all are aware of how we appear on social media (only positive stories and memorable photographs on Instagram, for instance), even without actually using avatars, and have a separate "public face" for each social platform that we inhabit.

At another level, this is about **re-defining community:** man is a social animal. We have always searched for communities, for belonging, for a sense of significance. Historically, this was limited by one's physical boundaries defined by the village or extended family. Now, with the internet and social media, this sense of "community" may extend across the globe. Witness the large tribe of people who fervently believe in the "flat Earth theory" or in the "alien creation" hypotheses, thereby creating a new "digital reality" prism through which they view the world. We will explore this theme more in the following discussion.

We see two key characteristics of this evolution in social identity:

A) Characteristic 1: our addiction to social media

Social media has gone from an interesting "curiosity" to stay in touch with old school friends to a tool that has become a fundamental part of the way we view ourselves and the way we live.

And this comfort with the use of social media to stay connected with family and friends has occasionally morphed into an "addiction", with its own resultant illnesses. Ranging from a reluctance to interact in the "real world" to envy of projected "ideal lifestyles" by people one is connected to on Instagram. At the extreme, this can lead to depression or other illnesses.

However, on the flip side, with the removal of physical barriers to interaction, we see a distinct evolution in the way society interacts.

The Covid crisis, resulting lockdowns, and "work from home" paradigms forced people to use and be comfortable with the use of technology to connect.

Seamless video sharing, which was already possible before Covid, has now gone mainstream.

As we go forward, these interactions will be enriched by technological innovations and may soon involve augmented and virtual reality, and possibly, holographic projections that simulate being in the same room.

Facebook and Microsoft have already demonstrated such technologies. Isaac Asimov wrote presciently a few decades ago about such technologies in his works of science fiction (the "Foundation series", now brought alive on the small screen by Apple TV!).

B) Characteristic 2: the outsize socio-political impact of social media (see box)

While the internet has brought much good to our lives, it has also amplified all that's going on around us. It seems that every single incident, everywhere on the planet, is reported in real time, 24/7.

One of the earliest illustrations of the power of social media to align and unleash vast social forces was the Arab Spring, which flared across North Africa a decade ago.

Nurtured and spread using Facebook, it put a lasting fear of social media into the minds of governments everywhere.

As a society, we are still coming to grips with the changes driven by the social media platforms that use this hyper connectivity. For the first time, no matter how extreme one's point of view, it is easy to find people with similar points of view on the internet.

Thus, most of us live in vast **echo chambers,** where we hear our prejudices echoed back to us. Thereby increasing extremism and intolerance and reducing possibility of dialogue, the world over.

The spirit of open and robust debate and discussion which was so much a part of the social revolution ushered in by a free press a hundred years ago, has now all but disappeared.

Elections are increasingly shaped by how one distorts or projects facts in social media. The possibility of meddling in elections to suit ones own agenda is no longer a luxury limited to well-funded intelligence agencies.

"There are no rules, no codes of conduct, and this world can feel oppressive and overwhelming", writes Anita Moorjani in her new book, *Sensitive is the New Strong.*

Even as traditional media increasingly offer one-sided analyses with a built-in bias, depending on their ownership or editorial political affiliations, people increasingly turn to social media for keeping track of the news.

This comes with its own challenges (see box for echo chambers).

In addition, a key challenge going forward, which governments and societies will now try to address, is how to identify "fake news". Perhaps we will use AI algorithms to systematically pre-screen everything we read and check it on Snopes.com.

Tech and the digital world have created a social revolution to **unleash the "Power of One"**. This has changed our identities and fundamentally altered social discourse, altered the concept of power (linked now to one's ability to influence people online), led to new, changed politics, and new ways of marketing and advertising.

The power of social media is something that successful politicians today understand too well. Presidents of the US have used Twitter to mobilise their supporters.

Irrespective of whether one is pro or anti this trend of direct outreach to one's support base, often with relatively hard line views, this trend is here to stay.

The future of elections, communications, and social views will increasingly be shaped by a "140 character tweet"!!

And this has potentially even changed the concept of "nationalism" as people discover their "tribes" (with common thinking patterns) extending across traditional national or state boundaries.

There is a dark side to this ubiquity of information access and sharing, especially as devices get connected online and share information constantly, without the users realising it: **the loss of privacy**. This access to data is increasingly being used by governments to keep an eye on "social undesirables". It is also inevitably being used by corporates to anticipate and even stimulate (dare one say "manipulate"?) demand creation. And, increasingly, by criminals trying to steal people's data to access their bank accounts or social security information. There is a great deal of justifiable concern in this area, though perhaps the most active privacy rights protection regimes are in Europe with the GDPR.

The implications are a new social discourse – a new way of engaging, influencing, and fulfilling. And a new way of engaging with markets, consumers, and audiences.

3. IMPLICATIONS FOR MARKETS AND MARKETPLACES

A) Marketplaces

The rise of the internet and social connectivity created unprecedented opportunities for enterprise as we saw web traffic in 1994 already grow at 2,300% per year!! (Ref.: various articles on Fleximize.com and other sites.)

In addition to Amazon (see box), which used the ubiquitous access and convenience afforded by the internet to disrupt traditional supply chains, we see the rise of platforms such as JD.com in China and e-bay in the US.

Alibaba (which allowed small, China-based enterprises to have global reach and marketing power) became a global powerhouse. And, on a smaller scale, copycats like Flipkart, Nykaa, and others in India gained rapid traction.

Each of them had a distinct proposition. A market place for businesses to sell to businesses. A market place for consumers who wished to re-sell. A market place for premium goods. Fashion (rent a runway). The internet made it possible to segment the purchase "need state" and create bespoke models that catered exclusively to that need state.

This shifted the balance of power away from traditional intermediaries like retailers (who used information arbitrage and their control on physical access) to consumers, providing them with almost unlimited access and information. Adoption has been exponential.

So, middlemen are disappearing unless they can add value beyond information arbitrage. This destroys some markets (the real estate broker) and also creates new ones (last-mile delivery).

Jeff Bezos, who was working on Wall Street at the time, saw the opportunity, and launched Amazon as **"the world's largest bookstore".** A concept not limited by the restricted physical space of traditional "brick and mortar" book stores.

The business saw explosive growth rates even he could not have imagined, as the company continued to plough everything back into growth.

Soon, the consumer database was so rich that Amazon could diversify into a vast array of products, and even services. Building customer intimacy and supply chain management as key competencies.

And **traditional bookstores** like Borders **went bankrupt...**soon, several stores in other categories followed suit.

Even Facebook offers a platform for sellers and buyers to come together. "Social commerce is about to go mainstream", says Millennial and e-commerce thinker Charu Misra in her article on Medium.

There is no sector left untouched. Physical goods. Services like education. And several others. This has been helped by the power of the internet to enable digital, cashless transactions through credit cards, payment portals, as well as rising, new digital payment services like PayPal. We will look more at these trends in the subsequent sections.

B) Opportunities for markets and enterprise

The disruptive change of the internet has inspired several new businesses, as startups were no longer limited by the traditional "retail power" of large, fast-moving consumer goods majors.

- New startups ("The Mom's Co" or "Mama Earth" in India) are mostly selling through e-commerce and bypassing expensive, traditional distribution networks. They get speed of access and scale of reach, which enables them to compete with established giants whose strength lies in dominating traditional distribution networks.

> **COVID** has accelerated **adoption of online shopping behaviour,** as lockdowns forced people to stay at home.
>
> **E-commerce boomed.** And fuelled several knock on benefits across industries…**courier and delivery services boomed.** Airlines like Emirates and Indigo pivoted to cargo to compensate for decreased passenger traffic.

- The rise of online global marketplaces created global access for small and medium enterprise. Building and maintaining trust and reputation are key in this space. Alibaba, as a platform, was key to the global outreach of Chinese SME and the economic export led boom that led to China becoming the "factory of the world".

- Similarly, B2B marketplaces.[3] For new equipment – even for second-hand factory equipment – one can now go online in specialised marketplaces and search for great "deals", thereby levelling the access to technology and equipment. Leading, in turn, to more disruptive new products created by emerging startups across the world.

C) The emerging big "data driven" marketplace shifts

- A key asset of business of the future is data. Ownership of the end consumer interface, relationship, and data. This allows personalisation as well as anticipation of emerging requirements. This comes with its own opportunities and challenges.

- We are quite happy to accept movie recommendations from Netflix or search recommendations from Google to improve our searches. However, as enterprise learns to aggregate, link, and use data, there is a growing concern that it may have too much access into our private lives.

- It was a decade ago that a major retail chain in the US – Target – was able to identify (based on purchase patterns) that a customer was pregnant and sent appropriate retail offers to her home . . . only to learn that she hadn't yet announced her pregnancy at home!

- Similarly, enterprises with access to data, like social media platforms, may "sell" this data to advertisers who use this to target and tailor their offers. There is a genuine and emerging concern for data privacy and protection. As discussed earlier in this chapter, regulations like the GDPR are designed to protect customer's access to data.

- Notwithstanding privacy related concerns, brands and marketers will need to move beyond ownership of physical assets (land, building, machinery, offices, etc.). These assets may well shift to aggregators who provide low-cost services. And into understanding data as a key asset.

- To quote KPMG,[4] "To capitalize on data as an asset, organizations will need to become more data driven – and data fluent. One promising accelerator toward data literacy is the explosion of 'citizen developers,' that is a business user with a blend of both business and technical acumen, rather than a traditional developer, who can create applications that generate business value".

D) Ratings and reviews are a key marketing tool

Gaetano Dinardi wrote in his Nextiva Blog in 2019: "When customers speak, brands listen". Monitoring and dealing with customer reviews is the entry price for doing business in a customer-centric economy. www.nextiva.com/blog/importance-of-customer-reviews.html.

Customer reviews have always existed in the form of "word-of-mouth" feedback, both good and bad, made to close friends. Now customers can go online to amplify their voice using social media and via customer review sites (like Google or Yelp or Booking.com or others). As a result, customers find it easy to share their experiences about a brand, both good and bad.

This provides them with a strong role in shaping brand reputation and determining the course of market share and repeat business evolution.

In addition, media routinely publishes online assessments by experts which dissect one's product and compare it to competition.

Brands and marketers are learning to pay close attention to monitoring these "ratings and reviews" and to address the root causes of customer dissatisfaction.

As a result, the more sophisticated BPO operations and call centres, which first came into existence as outsourced "complaint handling centres" are shifting away from "problem resolution" metrics to "advocacy" metrics, where one measures how many callers have actually been converted to brand advocates.

E) The power of "mass customisation"....

The pre-internet era was the era of "mass marketing". Henry Ford exemplified this best with his legendary statement, "You can have any colour you want provided it is black". Marketers catered to the largest viable consumer segment, and everybody had to fall in line or make do.

Now, however, the internet, and especially social media, access has created global "communities" of scale, with similar beliefs, who can represent a viable communication and business opportunity (targeted to a niche) hitherto too small to address within each geography.

It is possible, today, to log on to the website of a chocolate brand like Kitkat, and "design and print" a new chocolate label that incorporates the photo you upload. For a small fee therefore, one can create a "bespoke" gift of a chocolate designed specially for the receiver.

One can now aggregate niches across various geographical markets using social media and create a sizeable opportunity, which can be addressed via e-commerce.

Welcome to the era of "Mass Customization"!!

F) Media, entertainment, and digital marketing

We can expect an intensification of the effect of social media on society as penetration increases across populations. We already see news media, entertainment (TikTok and its clones), and advertising shifting away from traditional media towards social media.

The very way enterprise communicates has changed.

In the age of **"Mass Media"** in the 1990s and 2000s, most communication was "one to many", and one bought ads on prime time television or targeted programs while praying they would result in purchase.

We then migrated, with the advent of email and social media, to CRM and "one to one" marketing with targeted advertisements.

Today with e-commerce, (and mobile phone commerce) and people relying on ratings and reviews more than ever to vet their purchases, we have moved to the era of "many to many" communication.

Users share with each other content they like or recommend. They post on WhatsApp, Instagram, Facebook, and other social media sites. They praise, they criticise. They share. They rate. They review each offering and don't hold back. They "reward" companies whose stance on social or environmental issues mirrors what they believe in. And lead boycott calls on those who do not.

The task of the marketer now moves to be the "orchestra conductor" who curates this "live" conversation customers have about the brand. And 'seeds' content that is relevant to keep this conversation going. And engages in a conversational style that is not too serious or corporate.

Indeed, the very way that business advertises and connects with consumers, especially Millennials and Gen Z, is undergoing a major shift (see box).

And, more than ever before, media and marketing efforts will have to work very closely with sales channels on e-commerce and m-commerce to orchestrate conversations and seed appropriate content that leads to demand generation and actual purchase.

We will see the rise of the "buy now" button across all vectors of consumer contact. Consumers expect seamless connectivity and frictionless commerce. Wherever. Whenever.

4. IMPACT ON COMMERCE AND TRANSACTIONS

Cash will be but a distant memory as we migrate at warp speed into this internet-enabled economy demanded by Millennials and Gen Z (see box).

We will look in this section at tech-related commerce as a set of **two impact themes** that show the underlying change – and not just as a list of technologies. First, an impact on transactions. And thereafter, in the very concept of money. . . .

A) The underlying digital impact on transactions

i)   **Transactions are facilitated by the use of digital identities and technologies enabling secure, friction-free commerce with an anytime, anywhere convenience. These could be considered a foundational set of attributes.**

To start with, given the high penetration of mobile phones, wireless, and the internet, the phone becomes an ideal tool to transform and enable ease of transactions in business.

A fascinating story is the digital revolution in Kenya, where the introduction of digital transactions via MPesa led to transformation in society. According to the Economist magazine, already today, 25% of the economy in Kenya is digital. And mobile. Which makes them leaders in this emerging tech.

Consumers in Kenya can now pay for vegetables and fish in the fresh market using mobile payments. Or for a shoe shine service on the curb side. In the process, large numbers of people have access to digital financial services with which they can create new services in the economy.

This trend has spread since then to other markets. China has the ubiquitous "**WeChat**" app where customers can transfer money or conduct commerce. **WhatsApp** is experimenting with this payment feature now in India.

Google Pay, Apple Pay, Pay Pal, PayTM, and several other players have moved into the area of mobile payments. Many customers are people who never had a bank account in the past. Now, with "mobile commerce", they have leapfrogged into the 21st century. They have moved from the "informal", "cash" economy into the formal, digital economy

> **The Financial Express newspaper in India published in September 2021 some astonishing data from 2020:**
>
> According to the entrepreneur.com, India was home to the highest number of real time online transactions in 2020, with over 25 billion real time payments processed. Followed by China with almost 16 billion, South Korea with 6 billion, Thailand with 5 billion, the U.K. with almost 3 billion, and the US with 1.2 billion (ranked ninth) transactions.
>
> To be fair, this is a measure of "the number of transactions" and does not include a "value" metric per transaction. Still the sheer number of online transactions even in a country like India serves to highlight the speed of adoption of digital technologies for cashless transactions over the internet.
>
> **Watch this space......**

At the same time, with digital payments, the "cost" of financial transactions is dropping sharply.

What is the implication of this shift for enterprise? We can expect that the migration of large numbers of people from the "informal" economy into the "formal" economy will create significant new opportunities for enterprise.

In India, the government has enabled this shift (see box) with the introduction of the **UPI (Unified Payment Interface) initiative,** which provides anyone with a mobile phone seamless access to banking and related products.

In more developed economies, improved sensors and facial recognition engines have enabled the development of teller-less stores (Amazon) or vending machines.

As a result, transactions have become safe, secure, and are backed by regulatory controls that provide comfort to all players. In a similar vein, the cost of Forex transactions and remittances is dropping sharply and creating more purchasing power in the hands of the poor.

Some banks have transformed themselves, to ride and even help shape this digital wave.

DBS was a sleepy public sector bank in Singapore. In 2009, they hired a new CEO, Piyush Gupta. Working actively with the board, he drafted a strategic plan to **transform the bank** and make it "digital first".

For several years running, DBS has been recognised as the **"best digital bank in the world"** and "the best bank in the world".

---

ii) **Intelligence and digital technologies can deliver never-before benefits, adding value to transactions beyond lower cost and convenience.**

"Peer to peer lending" is a good example of new, emerging financial services which were not possible earlier, through the traditional banking sector. This has opened up a whole host of possibilities to use the power of the market to offer credit avenues for small businesses via unsecured loans which the banking sector was unable to process.

B) Welcome to the future of cashless commerce

Through history, mankind has used various tools to serve as currency. Sea shells. Brass and bronze coins. Paper currency. Gold. Silver.

In every case, there are three sets of people required to enable legitimacy of any currency. A buyer, a seller, and a provider cum guarantor of the underlying value of the currency. This last role has increasingly been played by central banks around the world.

Now, however, blockchain technology, which allows for distributed ledgers and transactional data security using AI based algorithms, has thrown up a revolutionary and intriguing possibility. Digital currency. Which can be transferred seamlessly and instantaneously, anywhere. Worldwide. And in a currency recognised, provided, and guaranteed by the "crowd".

At this point, apart from Bitcoin, there are several digital currencies on the market. These are actively traded. But the lack of government and central bank support (indeed their active discomfort as they see a loss of control) has meant these currencies are very volatile, and demand appears to be mostly speculative. Up to now.

The Chinese government was the first to announce a government-backed cryptocurrency. We expect other countries will follow or endorse some of the existing cryptocurrencies.

There are also intriguing possibilities with the potential "securitisation" of intellectual property. Apparently, now a creator of music can sell his content using a cryptocurrency designed for that very purpose. Similarly, other forms of intellectual property creation can be monetised in a global marketplace which eliminates the middleman.

We will discuss more in this theme of cryptocurrencies and blockchain in Chapter 11.

To recap the transformations:

- Digital cash and transactions powered by fin-tech and computational leaps like block chain have created vast, new opportunities for commerce. Transactions are fundamental to every economic activity. The disruptions in how we transact and e-commerce can therefore potentially impact every sector, bringing about vast change opportunities.

- The purveyors of money are impacted. We can foresee tumult in the world of finance and banks – a dominant pillar of enterprise which potentially will see huge disruption.

- New digital assets, like NFTs, are now tangible and tradable! Adding a further dimension of "reality" to the metaverse.

5. THE TRANSFORMATION OF LIFE SPACES AS THESE ARE MIRRORED IN THE DIGITAL WORLD

Life-spaces like health, education, or law and order/justice significantly shape human life.

In Chapter 6, we had seen (using education as one example) how these spaces and their institutions are being comprehensively unbundled and recreated by the twin forces of change.

On one hand, epochal shifts are re-imagining our society and "way of life", changing the role and context of sectors like education. And we also see how digital technologies are disrupting the traditional deliveries and paradigms of each space as it morphs with a mirrored existence in the metaverse.

Once again, we see education in itself is fundamentally transforming as people seek a "lifelong learning" model, which is the only way for an individual to stay abreast of the speed with which every facet of our lives is being transformed by technology.

Internet-based mobile connectivity also allows social entrepreneurs like **"Rocket Learning"**, a "not for profit" social enterprise in India, to assist parents with "at home" education and skill development over the smart phone. This kind of intervention in the vital pre school developmental years will serve to reduce the skill gap in school going children, between children from affluent backgrounds and those from economically disadvantaged sections.

The startup was judged one of the six global winners in 2021, in the Education category, at the MIT solve awards

The internet offers great potential for enabling universal access to education (see box) and skill development at relatively low costs. In the process, it may be a tool with an outsize multiplier effect across the economy, as subsequent generations have access to better-quality educational resources.

And, while we continue to use education as an example, many other pivotal sectors (health or entertainment, for instance) are being similarly transformed by technology. Far-reaching implications with heightened social impact can be seen with breakthroughs of

- Widespread access

- Superior benefit delivery relevant to our new digitally enabled world

- Often with lower delivery cost

We expect such areas will see several startups vie to create new business models and become one of the most exciting fields of investment, entrepreneurship, and also social impact over the next decade.

6. GOVERNANCE

In a similar manner, we see transformations starting to happen in governance models. We see three powerful forces driving the change:

- "Digital shifts" that transform governance and the delivery of services to citizens

- Government initiatives to stimulate digital transformation of economies (it is increasingly **the** primary driver of overall societal and economic development)

- Societal challenges of transition

A) Digital shifts used by governments to transform services

The underlying environment has changed, as citizens become better informed on global events. On human rights. On duties and responsibilities of the government. Thanks to the effect of digital technologies discussed earlier in this chapter.

Migration of people (a significant force in this century, as discussed in the chapter on demographics) helps raise

> The use of **electronic voting machines in India** is a key development in better governance.
>
> On the positive side, it has allowed the country to conduct democratic elections in the largest constituency on Earth, and do so with speed, transparency and efficiency in counting and result declaration.
>
> The flip side is the open question of whether this use of technology is safe or open to hacking.

awareness of better governance practices elsewhere and raises expectations from government, thereby creating a powerful incentive for change. And the world has more migrants than ever before, both legal and illegal. Legal migrants from India today number in excess of 35 million, have a "GDP" similar to the country, and remit moneys close to 5% of GDP each year!!

A related shift is simply because of greater numbers of people looking for better governance; while government budgets are constantly under pressure, governments everywhere are forced to look for better, faster, more efficient ways. Enter digital initiatives for better governance.

Similarly, the adoption of digital technologies in governance has meant the decentralisation of innovation, as each officer is empowered to use digital tools to innovate in his area of responsibility.

Governments have enabled regulations to facilitate this transition to digital governance tools.

An example is the internet facilitation's law like India's RTI (Right to Information Act). This law enables any citizen to access and view any government files or comments with respect to any request or application filed by him. As a result, bureaucrats cannot anymore just "sit on files" or pursue vendettas against complainants.

The transparency this has ushered in has led to a better resolution of issues, and with greater speed, as even India's much vaunted bureaucracy feels the pressure of public scrutiny.

Processing has been moved digital, to use computers rather than humans.

This simplifies transactions and eliminates middlemen. Today, electricity bills, phone bills, and water bills can be paid seamlessly, over the internet. Customer service requests, likewise, are seamlessly handled.

Ease of transaction and better customer service is a key driver to general adoption by the lay public.

B) Government policy and initiatives to drive digital

We draw upon India and work done by McKinsey[5] to identify some imperatives for government action:

i) Platforms for digital transformation, accelerated adoption

The "Aadhar Card" in India, which is a digital identity card for **1.2 billion** citizens and includes key biometric data, is the largest such tool in the world and perhaps an indication of the way forward elsewhere as well. The development of a national data stack, building on this data and connecting it to bank accounts, electoral identity, tax identity, driving license, road usage, services usage, insurance, medical care, etc., has enabled extensive use of direct-access digital tools like "direct cash transfers", mobile messaging, email, web pages, and self-service apps (to track Covid, for instance).

In a similar vein, with better access to digital banking, governments are better placed to initiate "direct transfers of money" to recipients. This has been used to good effect in several countries like Brazil, India, and elsewhere.

"Direct bank transfers" are enabled by digitalisation, thereby eliminating middlemen and increasing the effectiveness of government disbursements and paving the way for a possible seamless adoption of a "Universal Basic Income", a concept being hotly debated by economists and experimented with.

UPI (Unified Payments Interface) is a great example of a platform, initiated by the Indian government, which has resulted in exponential growth in digital transactions. ONDC (Open Network for Digital Commerce) is yet another initiative by the Indian government to create an accessible e commerce marketplace (albeit, unproven, as yet).

ii) Policies and investments: digital transformation for national transformation

Governments everywhere have realised their central role in creating and regulating digital infrastructure to ensure wide access, including to the underprivileged.

Policies that leverage public-private partnerships help stimulate infrastructure and encourage entrepreneurship and more rapid new business formation. This requires simplifying regulations, along with fiscal and other financial incentives. Speedy build-up of digital access and infrastructure is perhaps the most important driver of digital transformation and its cascade of economic benefits.

Entrepreneurs in India are already accessing the national data stack and access to create disruptive, new models of delivery of services, making India one of the hottest hubs for "startups".

Government policies also shape development of foundational industries like telecom. With accelerated developments, India "data costs" have plummeted to amongst the lowest in the world, even as usage has risen manifold.

Similarly, investment in human capital (re-thinking education, training, and learning) will have a profound impact on future economies.

iii) Regulatory frameworks/initiatives – e.g., GDPR, social media protocols, spectrum auction, etc.

Realising the enormity of this shift, governments are creating new regulatory frameworks to help monitor and regulate the "metaverse". These include access to new technologies like "5G". Or auction of data spectrums.

In a similar vein, governments are establishing sovereignty over data assets (all data on Chinese citizens has to be stored within the country, for instance). They are even creating and mining data on their own citizens (DNA registries, face recognition, etc.).

Indeed, one reason why cryptocurrencies are slow to get government endorsements has been the difficulty in regulatory oversight and transparency.

C) The challenges ahead

A major barrier to better use of these technologies in better governance has been the reluctance (or in some cases inefficiency) in sharing data transparently between databases. Certainly, this is the case between countries. And often even between different departments in the same country!! As this inefficiency is removed, digital governance will become smoother and more seamless. And simultaneously behave more like "Big Brother". . . . A sword that cuts both ways. . . .

Another key issue with increasing digital governance in large countries like India is the gap between "haves" and the "have nots". Between the digitally enabled, and the digitally illiterate. Sustained efforts will be needed to eliminate this gap, in the absence of which the fruits of better governance, enabled by digital tech, will also be unevenly distributed.

Further, to quote from McKinsey, "Even as digital growth is stimulated policy makers must evolve policies that help workers and institutions adapt to the impact on employment: Rethinking income support and safety nets. may need to be considered and tested".

In a new world, a re-imagination of governance is the need of the hour.

– – – – – – – –

To close this chapter, the new digital "virtual, digital reality" seems more and more to be a ubiquitous extension of the real world . . . and the road stretching ahead seems imbued with mystery and the power to enhancing and further fundamentally change our societal interactions and perhaps our very identity. . . .

As these **"virtual and augmented reality" technologies** get progressively more sophisticated, we start to question whether our current existential reality may itself be a computer simulation, much like the movie "The Matrix".

The scientist and noted spokesperson Neil deGrasse Tyson has said that it would be difficult to argue convincingly against this hypothesis!!

Indeed one of the striking things that have made video games so successful (an industry now several times larger than Hollywood) is that the outcomes are not predictable, but depend on the actions of the characters one "assumes" in an immersive reality experience. Thereby changing the experience each time one plays. And inviting the addiction to play again and again...

Welcome to the "Brave New World" (with respectful apologies to Aldous Huxley).

NOTES

1 Today, of the around 8 billion people in the world, approximately half are online. One in three people in the world use social media (over two-thirds of the people online). These numbers are huge – and growing!

2 Often, the 'metaverse' is viewed as a form of the next generation internet, a Web 3 framework, capable of heightened virtual reality experiences. We believe that there is an existing reality of consumer and social lives being in a metaverse, a virtual world. And such advancements represent just the next steps as this world becomes increasingly more "real" and important.

3 Here is a listing of B2B market places: www.nchannel.com/blog/top-b2b-marketplaces/.

4 https://assets.kpmg/content/dam/kpmg/xx/pdf/2019/10/data-as-an-asset.pdf

5 www.mckinsey.com/capabilities/mckinsey-digital/our-insights/digital-india-technology-to-transform-a-connected-nation

Chapter 9

The Addition of Intelligence
"Smart" Drives the Future

Experts are already predicting a future world driven by artificial intelligence.

However, most of us are still trying to figure out what AI even means. This is a technology that is expected to influence many aspects of our lives, from jobs to entertainment to health care. This may also raise fundamental questions about what it means to be human. Questions like "What is the nature of creativity?" and "How do we define consciousness?".

Posing the question "How can I understand AI?" is nearly as daunting as asking "What is the meaning of life?".

I. AI: FROM THE PAGES OF SCIENCE FICTION TO SHAPING A NEW REALITY

Artificial intelligence and **humanoids** have stirred human imagination for ages. Arthur C Clarke's and Stanley Kubrick's "2001: A Space Odyssey" – a movie released in 1968 – became a landmark film that captured the imagination of many people. The main antagonist in the film, HAL (Heuristically programmed, ALgorithmic computer), controls the systems of the spacecraft and interacts with the crew.

HAL has been shown to be capable of speech, speech recognition, facial recognition, natural language processing, lip reading, art appreciation, interpreting emotional behaviours, automated reasoning, spacecraft piloting, and playing chess. Science fiction then, but the capabilities depicted are surprisingly close to emerging reality today!

For decades, powerful machines which could surpass human capabilities seemed like developments which were around the corner. There were significant advancements with technology demonstrators for AI, such as "Deep Blue", the IBM initiative which demonstrated chess-playing capability and, in 1997, defeated the reigning world chess champion Gary Kasparov. However, for over four decades after this, there appeared little progress beyond these isolated events, and everyday lives remained seemingly untouched.

Today, however, AI has emerged from a long hibernation and is fast becoming ubiquitous. The first big applications of AI have been almost unobtrusive,

DOI: 10.4324/9781003254737-11

intelligent "engines" which understand us and shape everyday interactions. It is artificial intelligence that drives significant sections of our Facebook experience, our Google searches, or even the buying suggestions on our favourite online market places. **Virtual assistants, Siri and Alexa, are a vocal embodiment of AI**.

AI applications are emerging in a host of industries. AI is already starting to become the differentiator and is even leading the industry agenda in some (e.g., autonomous cars). Business value created by AI has increased exponentially (estimated in 2025 at $118 billion).

So, while some of our most valued companies have embraced AI (and many startups are racing off the blocks using it), it is a buzz word that is not much understood.

A McKinsey study shows that most business leaders are aware of it being on the horizon, but over 80% are really not sure of what to do with it in their businesses. What's more, a separate Accenture study shows that 80% of executives feel that they would lose out on competitive opportunities if they do not act fast to use this.

It is not the objective of this chapter to delve into the huge and rapidly growing technical foundations of artificial intelligence. (In our reference section, however, the reader will find a shortlist of excellent articles which, in a simple way, but insightfully, introduce us to the different facets of this space.)

Our focus is on understanding the essence, and impact of AI. What is it and what makes it powerful? And how can it change our lives and the world of business?

And as we understand its genesis and see its power, we start to sense why "artificial intelligence" possesses the potential to transform our future.

2. UNDERSTANDING ARTIFICIAL INTELLIGENCE

• The "addition of intelligence" – a progressive journey

Knowledge and ideas have long shaped civilisation. Early human progress, including the use of tools and agriculture, was powered by human intelligence, sometimes ingenuously supplemented by the energy of domesticated animals and nature.

With the Industrial Revolution, new technology and ideas developed. Mechanisation driven by steam or electricity helped execute tasks with higher productivity, but the intelligence directing these tasks was still largely human.

The surge in computerisation in the 20th century signalled the start of another revolution: one which input "intelligence" (based on past data and predetermined analyses) to facilitate computations and drive speedier outcomes.

Technology and advances in miniaturisation have now enabled these powerful computers to reside inside our "smart phones". The introduction of "apps" in 2007 allowed us to access (literally with our fingertips) this intelligence and computational ability, thereby simplifying its application to everyday activity.

• Artificial intelligence (AI): the new frontier

The addition of intelligence is taking a leap ahead, once again, with artificial intelligence (AI).

Artificial intelligence is different from passive intelligence which can provide only predetermined responses.

In its essence, these software systems "make decisions which normally require a human level of expertise" and help people anticipate problems or deal with issues as they come up. As such, they operate in an intentional, intelligent, and adaptive manner.[1]

They draw upon real-time data from diverse sources: digital inputs or sensors or even fuzzy data with incomplete information. Advanced computational abilities make AI capable of tremendous power in drawing out insights for decision making.

Not only does AI mimic human thinking, AI applications can learn from experience, which will allow them to adapt to situations and improve steadily over time.

THE FOUNDATIONS OF AI

What is AI?

Learns from data (lots of it!) **and delivers human level of expertise** (or even better)

- AI is driven by **powerful computational models** and **algorithms**
- Enabled by **connectivity + data + sea of technologies**

What makes it powerful

INTENTIONAL
using real time inputs

INTELLIGENCE
synthesising complex decisions

ADAPTIVE
self learning, swarm learning

• The disruptive difference: AI applies human-like intelligence, magnified manifold

The human difference in any action is "intelligence". AI applies "human-like" intelligence to actions. So, for example, when AI is applied to grading apples, it does not do so merely based on size. Like human beings, it could apply "human-like" intelligence to assess colour, shape, softness, or a host of similar attributes. And hence, sort apples better.

AI can apply not just average "human-like" intelligence, but **expert** human intelligence. AI-enhanced radiology scans detect tumours by drawing upon the accumulated experience of world-class specialists.

What's more, AI systems need not merely draw upon human knowledge but can acquire knowledge adaptively. Concepts like swarm learning and machine learning[2] are significantly multiplying capabilities; they can train the application to learn from data by itself and accomplish future tasks better.

AI systems, of course, have the characteristic advantage of machines: to work ceaselessly, even in inaccessible places and with a consistency unmatched by humans!

3. MULTIFACETED BENEFITS, MANY TECHNOLOGIES, MANY DIMENSIONS

AI applications can apply intelligence in diverse and powerful ways, often enabled by supporting technologies. Not only are these evolving opportunities for companies to significantly enhance performance; they are disruptively changing consumer expectations and business operations.

We look at some of the game-changing themes that are impacting our world and the possibilities in the future.[3]

A) Assisted living: facilitated by AI

AI can interface with consumers to better understand their context and intelligently provide them with tailor-made responses or solutions. Advancements in voice and image recognition have enabled people to "talk" to machines effortlessly, and this drives rapid adoption of "assisted living".

Suggestions for shopping, reading, and many more everyday activities are often welcomed (though not without some discomfort at their intrusiveness). Virtual assistants and smart home systems are our new aides.

Assisted living extends into routine chores. Take, for example, robot vacuum cleaners like "Roomba" or equivalent lawn mowers and even pool cleaners. Or the smart phone, which can notice if one falls and send alerts for help.

B) Robots: changing how the world does things

In science fiction, AI was often associated with robots and visualised as humanoid machines that could autonomously perform tasks.

Today, AI is providing all kinds of machines with increased capability to assess unstructured environments and act autonomously. Equipped with "better than human" precision, ability, and power, they also often can do jobs considered as hazardous for people – or ones where ennui or exhaustion can lead to poor quality.

We may not notice today's robots (given their nonhumanoid appearance!), but in diverse forms and domains, they are changing the way the world does things.

Cheaper and better robots are being rapidly adopted in factories. Advances in their ability to learn enable them to improve over time.

Pilotless planes, ships, and "drones" used in war are salient examples of autonomous machines. And, as our parallel digital world takes shape, sophisticated bots of the metaverse power actions there too. For instance, AI-based trading is today disrupting financial markets.

C) Micro-segmentation

Micro-segmentation of consumers – and customising products and promotions – is not only one of the biggest commercial applications of AI. It is changing the way customer needs are being fulfilled by large companies like Facebook, Google, or Amazon, as well as by startups.

A compelling example is the use of AI by consumer finance companies to form extremely precise, targetable segments. And with the insights generated, they can generate a higher productivity in customer acquisition, make better decisions of the right loan amount, as well as reduce the credit risk. These are the primary determinants of their competitive advantage and business profitability.

Marketing budgets are becoming more productive. Micro-segmentation with AI is helping companies expose consumers with customised stimuli and offers. Effectiveness improves dramatically as the stimulus intelligently adapts to specific individual, **in real time!** Large-scale, evidence-based decision making and insights are leading to competitive advantages in acquiring and retaining customers longer.

Customisation is the new paradigm and AI powerfully enables it, at scale.

D) The new efficiency is "smart"

AI-based systems are driving efficiency by promoting better capacity utilisation, forecasting, matching of supply and demand, etc. New developments in the **"internet of things" (IoT)** and sensors are enabling large-scale process efficiencies. With "always-on" artificial intelligence, quality assurance can check each unit rather than just sample a few batches.

Intelligence-based solutions are the smart, new normal. Smart grids are optimising electricity networks. Smart cities are using intelligence to deliver better solutions with lesser and more sustainable resources.

E) AI helps build new knowledge

AI not only impacts our decisions and actions but can even change how we create new knowledge.

Advances in AI are helping new developments in massively complex domains like pharmaceuticals, aerospace, or even weather forecasting. Automated algorithms help new discoveries that otherwise would not have been possible or would need significant human resources.

F) AI advancements and new horizons

Advances in AI are emerging every day. Developments in techniques like deep learning and reinforcement-learning based on neural networks is driving computational advances, the prime engine of AI. Artificial Narrow intelligence (ANI)[4] is already here. Artificial General Intelligence (AGI) promises to be here tomorrow.

If technology is the engine, the fuel for AI is data. Vast amounts of data are being generated in our increasingly digitised and connected world. The internet of things will help increase this further. AI technologies use this data to add value (see Appendix).

Breakthrough new products are emerging as large opportunities. With applications of ANI, "self-driving" cars are today a reality. New computational models like block chain can now be leveraged to create enterprise applications and value.

AI has potentially **a ubiquitous canvas**, ranging from the mundane to the sublime – from sorting apples to detecting tumours! And strong enablers are rapidly widening its impact.

- Automating the creation of AI itself will have a profound impact. Faster and cheaper development of AI can enable its application across a variety of domains, including small or simple applications like automating an intelligent chatbot.

- The cloud and high-speed connectivity are changing access to digital solutions. Data and high-powered algorithms can be cloud-based and the outcomes made available to individual or disaggregated users. It is estimated that a majority of applications would migrate to the cloud over the next decade, enhancing the ability to add intelligence to everyday tasks.

Equally in our digital metaverse, sites are getting re-imagined with AI. E-commerce sites which started as transaction portals today have intelligence-based suggestion engines. Intelligence is directing the operations of various banking interactions, ensuring credit evaluation and cyber-security.

Today, the three "streams" of connectivity, the metaverse, and "added intelligence" are fusing into one connected, intelligent metaverse. Intelligence is pervading through and the reach of AI-based solutions is almost limitless.

- As more people use AI in creative and effective ways, this has a domino effect: word-of-mouth generates excitement, experimentation, and accelerated adoption.

4. AI TECHNOLOGIES: A FUNDAMENTAL IMPACT ON ENTERPRISE AND SOCIETY

We see AI deliver powerful new benefits; however, it is the fundamental changes AI is triggering in our world that multiplies its disruptive impact, perhaps more than any other technology. We look at three foundational shifts:

A) The new world of data

We are inexorably moving to a new world of data. Data is exponentially increasing and is becoming the central force driving enterprise (see Appendix).

The new realities of data for businesses

- Data and intelligence-based analyses are powering conventional businesses with product and process improvement opportunities, as we have seen earlier in this chapter.

- Today, it's a world of connected consumers, who, with virtually every "life stroke", are generating data and expressing their demand. Businesses are being compelled to engage at each such moment, to understand consumers, and deliver better. Enterprise digital systems are being transformed to become consumer focussed (from an earlier focus on business transactions and internal process efficiencies).

> **FOUR CHALLENGES FOR ENTERPRISE IN THE WORLD OF DATA**
>
> 1) How does the company re-imagine its business in the world of "data"?
>
> 2) What are the company's choices-its "data" strategy, and advantage? Its product, process and strategic actions.
>
> 3) How to convert data into intelligence and build actionable value? How to monetise it?
>
> 4) What are the new competencies of "intelligent" business. How to build them?

- The end consumer perceives low value for data and is, perhaps, also overwhelmed by it. However, use of data and AI can add significant value, such as in consumer targeting and acquisition. Consumer-facing companies are, hence, emerging as big markets for such data and intelligence solutions. Data intelligence-based companies are seizing this opportunity, often with B2B models. Value is migrating to products which help extract incremental consumer advantage, and as a result, a large, upstream but consumer-centric value chain is developing. Analytics companies, cloud platforms, and even giants like Meta and Google are part of this.

- Enterprises are already being valued on their data assets – e.g., digital health companies add valuation as they access more patient data sets to better train their AI engines. Similarly, building a data edge to the business is becoming an imperative for almost every progressive enterprise (e.g., by developing a data-based revenue stream of significance or using data-based business models that enable better revenues). The key challenge is how to derive intelligence from data, to add actionable value, and thereafter, how to monetise it.

• Analytics and AI are becoming the new engines of business value creation. And artificial intelligence harvests its advantage from the use of data – lots of data. Data has, hence, become the critical resource which powers strategic advantage for enterprise.

Data and governance

Value creation and privacy concerns are coming together to make data an important centre point of global economic tussles and regulation. As data generates value, control on national data, its security, and utilisation are a national priority. Local siting of servers is seen as essential. Businesses can create data-based business value across national boundaries, raising questions on geographic taxation of such income. Governments are negotiating taxation protocols for this new world of data. The GDPR legislation by the EU is a trendsetter in the protection and use of data. Increasingly, "data" capabilities are seen as infrastructure and as a critical element of developmental priorities for governments in the new world.

B) Livelihood

Disruptive technologies, almost by their very definition, get widely adopted and significantly impact everyday life. And, as they shape our lives, a new set of embedded societal and ethical issues arise from this change. Labour movements arose out of the Industrial Revolution. Privacy issues are already centre stage with the rise of social media and consumer profiling for commercial advantage. Developments in laws, regulatory frameworks, and societal norms and institutions engage with such issues to facilitate a harmonious transition to a new way of living.

AI adds human-like intelligence to do human-like tasks (and more) even better. As it does, questions arise on what will humans do. And also, the purpose and supremacy of human life. The surge of AI is bringing into focus the very centrality of human life: jobs, livelihoods, and the human purpose.

AI would have a significant impact by automating many repetitive tasks and jobs. A McKinsey[5] study estimated that about half of the activities performed in jobs today are substitutable by adapting currently demonstrated technology.

But AI does not just make human jobs redundant. AI advances also cover areas not undertaken today – e.g., credit analysis or customer segmentation. Many expect that, while AI-based efficiency would impact jobs, new, richer roles would emerge and minimise the impact on livelihoods. Gary Kasparov,[6] the world chess champion, says, "Jobs don't disappear, they evolve. Deleting people from repetitive jobs frees them up to be more creative".

Nevertheless, we believe significant challenges exist as we transition to a world increasingly driven by AI. The speed of change may leave a gap in the near term.

Some segments of society may suffer in the transition more than others – lower-paid workers, especially. New skill sets will need to be built in an accelerated way.

Earning one's livelihood has been central to human life. But changes could be underway. Social support may become permanent and ideas like Universal Basic Income (UBI) could become the scaffolding holding up the well-being of societies. Consider also Dr. Eban Escott's[7] observation that, as bots take care of the heavy lifting, AI will bring what people want most: time. Less time working; more time living.

Along with UBI as a foundation, this may see a slow shift towards a society where livelihood ceases to be the primary driving force in our lives. And "living" takes centre stage!

One thing is for sure: that, as the world hurtles ahead, concerted thought and action would be needed to guide and shape this transformation by AI.

C) The frontiers of intelligence

In its journey to be more powerful and relevant, AI has become better at mimicking human beings. In many cases, AI is surging ahead of human capabilities. Given that human beings think and are conscious, will advanced AI make the leap to consciousness? What will be the impact of that? Is there a zone beyond human thought? Could AI go there? Answers to these questions will impact our societies and businesses.

Note: since we wrote the first draft of this book, ChatGPT has now burst onto the world, spreading at warp speed to all corners. It is so useful and versatile, that it threatens (promises?) to disrupt almost every field of human endeavour, whether it be teaching, research, doing medical diagnoses, or drafting legal contracts. The future is here. The only choice we have is to work with it and weave it into our lives and professions.

5. OUR TAKEAWAY

The application of human-like intelligence is a step change, changing fundamentally the way consumers and organisations do things. Rapid advances are bringing new breakthroughs and an ever-widening sphere of impact, showcasing the power and possibilities of AI.

As authors, we cannot envisage even one domain that cannot be positively impacted by AI. Because intelligence is at the heart of every intended human action. The application and impact of AI is limited only by our imagination. As leaders of change and opportunity, we need to engage with the technologies and applications of AI. And shape the actions that can transform our world.

We believe that AI can indeed become the biggest engine of disruption, perhaps even more than imagined by science fiction.

The future is intelligent.

NOTES

1   The definition of a complex area like AI can have multiple nuances. We draw from Shubhendu and Vijay to capture its essence. "Applicability of Artificial Intelligence in Different Fields of Life".

2   **Machine learning** enables applications to learn from their data sets and progressively improve with experience, without pre-given instructions. So, a factory robot can be trained to learn and improve, even as it works on site.
    Swarm learning is inspired by nature (think of coordinated movement of migratory birds!). It applies AI at distributed data points and helps draw out insights for the aggregated system. Applications are multiplying in areas like transport systems and health care.

3   Vast possibilities exist beyond our illustrations, given the inherent versatility of application of intelligence. Equally, the rapid progress of AI technologies necessitates continuous scanning for advancements and new inspiring applications.

4   Artificial Narrow Intelligence (ANI) is the ability to do clearly defined tasks in a narrow context – e.g., sort out fruits, play chess, or financial trading. Most of the AI applications today are ANI.
    Artificial General Intelligence (AGI) is when AI's ability is indistinguishable from humans in a multifaceted manner.
    And, Artificial Super Intelligence (ASI) is when AI surpasses human abilities at all ways, perhaps even including things like writing music, diagnosing ailments, etc. AGI abilities could be around the corner, but ASI, even today, seems like science fiction!

5   A detailed analysis of the impact of AI and automation on jobs can be found here: www.mckinsey.com/featured-insights/digital-disruption/whats-now-and-next-in-analytics-ai-and-automation

6   Gary Kasparov, the world chess champion, contested against IBM's Deep Blue computer in 1997. A landmark AI development, where a machine beat the reigning world chess champion for the first time.

7   Dr **Eban Escott** is the founder of Codebots, a technology platform where you can train **bots** to write code. The following article offers a perspective on Ai and its future impact. https://codebots.com/artificial-intelligence/the-3-types-of-ai-is-the-third-even-possible

8   As an example, in India, the average monthly internet data usage has increased from 1.24 GB per month in 2018 to 14.1 GB in 2021 (as per the Economic Survey 2022). This consumption promises to grow exponentially with the enhanced adoption of smart phones, the advent of new technologies like 5G, and as connected living and practices like work from home take root.

Appendix
The New World of Data

(We step back and look at what's driving the new world of data. Perhaps apt at this point of the book, as we round off our trilogy of chapters on the digital transformation.)

> **"The representation of a life reality in a numeric form. And with it, the ability to store & preserve the reality, transmit it, process or amplify it and use it for enhanced action."**
>
> An example-a picture, a purchase action or even a lingering look can be digitally captured at the moment. And can be shared, processed to understand preferences and drive purchase actions.

Digitisation, a powerfully simple concept **(see box),** is at the heart of our transforming world.

Breakthrough new technologies and societal applications, in many disruptive ways, are multiplying the force of digitisation to build a pervasive new world of data:

1) **UBIQUITOUS CONNECTIVITY** (with smart phones and high speeds) and adoption of a life in the metaverse has taken "digital" to the heart of consumer lives.

The consumer is generating giant streams of data as he or she lives in the digital world: a search, a purchase, a message – everything has a data signature. Virtually every interaction, everything done, every life stroke now has data. It is connected and can be processed for significant advantage.

New areas are getting digitised; for example, handwriting recognition systems are enabling digitisation of medical prescriptions.

New platforms – like for digital payments – and new applications like virtual assistants are emerging. Each enabling a higher level of data generation, intelligent analysis, and versatile actions to deliver benefits. Often collaboratively between multiple players.

IoT will multiply this as connected devices gain ground. Without even a mainstream application today, IoT data already exceeds the human stream and is likely to become many times more in the near future.

Useful and disruptive applications are powered by digitisation, and in turn, generate mountains of data.[8] Not just any data, but valued information with the embedded signatures of human life and needs.

2) **IN PARALLEL, ADVANCES IN ANALYTICS AND ARTIFICIAL INTELLIGENCE ARE MAKING THE APPLICATION OF DATA EXPONENTIALLY MORE VALUABLE.**

Insightfully discerning the signatures of consumer life and applying intelligence back to deliver superior actions and benefits. Most industries are likely to go through a three-step journey and get "digitally powered" – a migration from an analogue reality is the first step of the journey. Analytics add the next layer of insights, and AI applications follow as reliable data becomes readily available. Increasingly, enterprises can leapfrog and seize AI-based advantages, as is being seen in health care today.

In the past, data was largely transactional or demographic (often collected through transactions). Today, data is about life behaviours taken at the moment of life. Such richer, more voluminous data sets can provide a much larger variety of actionable insights for enterprise.

3) **A VIRTUOUS CYCLE IS FORMING** between the prolific availability of data and its application, generating more value and more data. **The new world of data and intelligence is fast expanding and shaping every aspect of society,** be it commercial domains or life-spaces like health and education; governance or even leisure and the arts. Further, strong, data-based inter-connections are developing, becoming the primary link between domains as diverse as media, markets, and money (as consumers, we can visibly see this in the case of our social media browsing, purchase pop-ups, and online financing offers!).

In this chapter, we have seen glimpses of some salient opportunities and implications for enterprise. We have also seen the implications for societies and governments, and in fact, on the fundamental purpose of human life.

And while the complexity makes it difficult to predict the future, we believe we are at an inflexion point. **A rapid transformation to a life in the new world of data.**

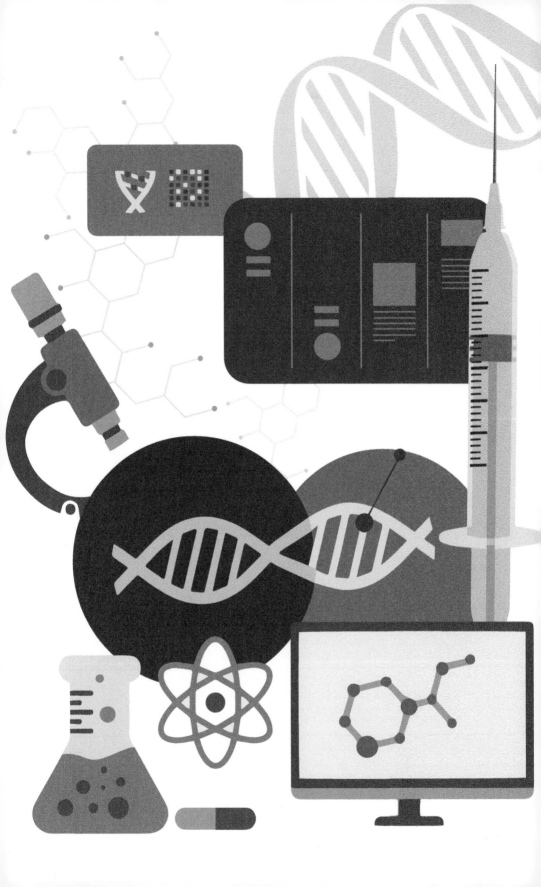

Chapter 10

The Revolution in Life Sciences
Health Is the Real Wealth

"It is health which is real wealth, and not pieces of gold and silver",
– Mahatma Gandhi

"Let food be thy medicine and medicine be thy food",
– Hippocrates, 400 BC

Following on from the earlier chapters about connectivity, the internet revolution and added intelligence. Here, we will explore the no less dramatic changes in the area of health care.

Health care is unique as an area which has an impact on business and society way beyond the direct costs or revenue attributable to the specific sector. A healthier society means a more productive and engaged workforce, whether in agriculture, industry, or the services sector.

And dramatic improvements in the application of changes in the physical sciences and technology in the form of genetics, stem cell research, and much, much more promises a revolution. The value creation effect in health care has effects which ripple through all sectors of the economy. This is an opportunity for enterprise as well as governments and political leadership.

CONTEXT

Since the dawn of civilisation, humanity has lived with the spectre of the horsemen of the apocalypse. One among them, "disease" has plagued us forever. We were always at war, trying to survive in the face of a world where every organism fights to make a place for itself.

Surviving meant staying healthy, overcoming threats to our health from three sources:

1. **Attack and infection by external parasites, fungi, bacteria, viruses, and prions.**

2. **Ageing and the wearing out of body parts or organs, often accelerated by lifestyle, poison, or diet.**

3. **Accidents or violence caused by animals or humans.**

DOI: 10.4324/9781003254737-12

Our response to each of these challenges is evolving, providing us with new understanding and technologies; and in the process, transforming health care and related businesses. The effects of these changes will cascade through the economy.

We will start by looking at the overarching impact of technology on health care models and then examine each of the health threats just listed. You will also discover how developments in related areas of physical sciences, like nanotechnology and 3D printing, have a flow-through impact as they find application in health care.

I. LIFE SCIENCES AND TECHNOLOGY

The application of technological developments to the realm of health care has the potential to create disruptive services and care models in large, diverse ways and at scale.

This impacts fundamentally the way we live and the way our societies develop.

Covid -19 has been a sobering wake up call, not only in its impact on health, but in its impact on the economy.

This has created great awareness of the impact of life sciences on financial issues as well as business.

Thanks to government investments, mRNA vaccines were developed on a vastly accelerated timeline. And societies have seen the benefits of vaccination benefit the entire economy, outweighing the costs.

The disease has been a compelling real life case study on the importance of health care and it's widespread effects. Effects which go beyond the increased value for the pharma companies involved in vaccine creation; societies which have high vaccination rates have seen the economies recover sooner with beneficial outcomes for all businesses, large and small.

We can see this happening along three sub-dimensions (a, b, and c, as follows):

A) The potential of technology to introduce concepts of preventative health

It is perhaps axiomatic in medicine that the earlier one treats an illness, the better the chances of a cure. And now, with technology. . . .

The future of medicine may be to treat illnesses even before they occur!!

The earliest concepts of treating illnesses consisted of interventions via diet, plant medicine (for example, the bark of the willow tree or quinine from the cinchona tree), or animal products after the illness had happened. These have been further refined by modern pharmaceutical companies.

Huge advances are also being made at understanding root causes of chronic diseases like cancer and systematically eliminating environmental triggers (smoking, pesticides, heavy metals, radiation, and materials like asbestos, etc.) as well as new techniques to target and treat cancers successfully.

Likewise, surgical interventions across a whole array of conditions have improved tremendously in effectiveness with the development of greater understanding and application of technology.

In this context, perhaps one of the most significant (and as yet under-rated) developments in health care has been the development of sensors and other wearable devices which can be linked via Bluetooth to smart phones. The smart phone is a powerful computer with great memory, communication, and processing power, available at our fingertips and accessible at all times.

Wearables like Fitbit, Nike, or the Apple Watch or equivalents monitor activity (number of steps), heart rate, sleep patterns, temperature, blood oxygenation levels (popularised by Covid), and, at an advanced stage, even blood pressure and blood sugar. This technology using non-invasive techniques will soon evolve to monitor other markers in the blood and body as well.

Linked to one's smart phone and continuously able to monitor and provide data feeds (and monitored by AI to detect patterns), an alert can be shared with the user as well as the health care practitioner.

> An interesting thought experiment imagines a day in your life in the year 2035.
>
> You have sensors attached permanently to your body, either as an attachment or as a pill you swallow, which non-invasively monitor your health parameters 24/7, and are linked via blue tooth to your PDA. Which in turn is connected via the internet to your doctor who practices telemedicine.
>
> Preliminary diagnosis is done by AI, which matches your basic health parameters to known illnesses and population statistics for your age and gender profile. This replaces the role of the GP and prepares a preliminary diagnosis.
>
> You get then on your PDA a message to modify your lifestyle or diet to proactively manage your blood or gut bacteria markers. You doctor is kept informed.
>
> If that fails to remedy the situation, you will receive a notification on your PDA to consult with a specialist, say a cardiologist, or an oncologist, initially over a video chat to review your markers. And then only perhaps an in-person visit to address the situation with drugs and or other treatment regimens.

The box alongside describes what seems a science fiction scenario but is, in fact, not far from what is today realistically possible.

It is perhaps difficult to imagine at first, but the development of the smart phone may be the most significant advance in health care since the Hippocratic oath was invented.

This is also helping change the health care insurance industry. Insurance companies in several countries now routinely offer free monitoring devices

> In a more futuristic vein, we have all marvelled at some point at the incredible **"Star Trek" technology** whereby "Bones" or Dr Leonard McCoy is able to use a handheld brain scanner to assess head injuries.
>
> This technology is now a reality, with the **"infra scanner"** being deployed by the US Marine Corps as the first portable handheld assessment tool. Science fiction now meets reality!!

and lower premiums to people who voluntarily sign up for a model that varies their premium based on their activity levels, thereby incentivising healthier lifestyles.

As we systematically address issues of disease, and thereby increase longevity, a number of researchers are setting their sights on a hitherto undreamt-of goal. . . . To tackle mortality itself!!

This raises several philosophical and religious questions, which we will not look at in this book but are worthy of discussion and debate.

B) The ubiquity of access created allows instant consultation and diagnosis through telemedicine

Access to the internet has prompted the evolution of telemedicine, which allows people to consult doctors for an opinion remotely.

Telemedicine-based models may perhaps revolutionise primary care across parts of Africa and South Asia, where physical health care infrastructure is insufficient (see box). This is a large and fast-growing new opportunity for health care business.

The internet has also democratised access to large amounts of literature on symptoms and treatments of most illnesses.

> A quick Google search reveals several fast growing companies offering consultation. Companies like Teledoc, "Doctor on Demand", "Amwell", "MDLiveCare"…in almost every country we can see similar startups creating and occupying this fast growing niche.
>
> Once legal and regulatory frameworks evolve, such companies could offer affordable primary consultation across borders, thereby creating significant impact on health care and society.
>
> We see this area is likely to attract more players and investment. It will also likely use AI to do preliminary screening to make the physician's job of diagnosis easier.

A cautionary note

This brings with it inevitably the dangers of self-diagnosis. . . . As every doctor will testify, patients come armed to the consultation with internet research and a prior "quasi medical" opinion on what their ailment is!

Hopefully this does not hurt the growth of telemedicine.

C) Creation of lifestyle support groups that share and encourage best practices

To paraphrase Dr Agus (ref.: the book *A Short Guide To a Long Life*), the best way to treat an illness is to avoid getting ill.

There is a growing realisation of this truism as society focuses more on the prevention of disease. Putting this truism into practice may involve actions like control of mosquitoes/disease vectors or social distancing and masking

(Covid-19) or changes in lifestyle to prevent many non-communicable diseases like a cardiovascular disease, diabetes, or other illnesses.

Additionally, as people start to make lifestyle changes to treat the whole body/ mind, rather than focus only on the symptoms of disease, they seek guidance, help, and reassurance from qualified doctors, nutritionists, as well as peers who have embarked on a similar journey. It is not easy to make dramatic changes in lifestyle, as anybody who has tried to go on a diet will attest. Here is where peer support groups become important.

There are several startups offering "apps" that assist with lifestyle choices. "Head-space" is a popular app for meditation; similarly, there are apps for sleep, apps for dieting, intermittent fasting, exercising, running. The list is almost endless.

> We have seen an **explosion of startups creating apps** that reside on your smartphone or PDA and offer support groups to help manage disease. These support groups may even be sponsored by pharma companies or hospitals.
>
> A quick Google search will reveal dozens of apps available for just about every disease and disorder. It is easy to join these groups for free, or even for a nominal charge.
>
> They are useful in information sharing and community building in search of health specific applications, and are as varied as they are creative.
>
> For example, the startup, Fooya (Wikipedia) is a medical mobile app which uses gamification to induce children to improve their diet and lifestyle. With extensive clinical studies in partnership with noted medical institutions like Johns Hopkins, and others, they aim to help create a childhood "digital vaccine" to prevent unhealthy habits from developing!!

This is a huge, fast-growing, and emerging business opportunity that we see many startups entering and creating value in. And an opportunity which may create myriad new opportunities for business and for coaches.

2. ATTACK AND INFECTION BY EXTERNAL PARASITES, FUNGI, BACTERIA, VIRUSES, AND PRIONS

We now have a better understanding of how human mechanisms have evolved over time to respond and survive in the face of repeated threats from pathogens.

Over millennia, starting from the origins of life itself in the shallow, warm oceans, life has involved struggle – a competition for resources – as each organism is simultaneously hunter and the hunted.

Over time, the human body evolved its defences against these attackers both by co-opting bacteria in a symbiotic alliance and by building robust immune responses which ensured genes that survived and evolved to cope with infection.

In recent times, the pharmaceutical industry has refined techniques with industrial-scale research and "manufacture at scale" of specific molecules targeted at specific illnesses. Witness the fabulous effort of Merck at helping control and cure river blindness in Africa by isolating an anti-parasite molecule from a

Japanese soil sample to create the drug Ivermectin, which they then gave away free!! (See box.)

Much effort, however, is now being devoted to targeting and controlling the disease vectors in the first place. And hope exists that we may be able to use genetically engineered mosquitoes to control mosquito-borne diseases. These are incredible applications of technology to rid us of diseases humanity has carried for millennia.

In addition, there is, today, a growing awareness of the importance of the "second genome": the billions of bacteria which exist (mostly in our gut) in a complex ecosystem of species in a symbiotic alliance with the host human. We could call this the "**second genome**" – the microbiome moderating human health.

It appears we live in a symbiotic relationship with bacteria and

---

An interesting and inspiring study we often discuss in B-School is that of **Merck.**

In 1978, researchers at the company discovered that a veterinary drug, ivermectin, (discovered after a laborious process involving analysis of soil samples from all over the world), also offered the potential to fight the parasite, onchocerciasis volvulus, which was spread by tiny black flies, and could cause **river blindness.**

This was a debilitating disease affecting thousands of Africans with no known cure at the time. Commercial development was risky, because the affected countries and populations were unlikely to ever be able to offer a viable financial return.

Eventually Merck decided to develop the drug and offer it for free. This helped control a dangerous disease in vulnerable populations in Africa. The effort was recognised in 2015 when the company researcher William C. Campbell, now retired, was awarded the Nobel Prize in Physiology.

Technology and painstaking research combined with international efforts have helped eradicate diseases such as small pox, polio, and and several other historical scourges

---

viruses which have evolved with us. There is still debate on exact numbers, but it appears we may harbour ten times the number of bacteria as the number of human cells in our body. And apparently, 90% of these live inside our gut in a complex ecosystem. Thousands of species of bacteria live in a complex balance in different parts of our digestive tract (see box).

There is a growing realisation that this "bacterial fingerprint" may be our "second genome", which modulates our health in an as-yet-incompletely-understood dance with our genetics.

Perhaps, instead of indiscriminately killing off gut bacteria with antibiotics, it is time to start thinking of how to use bacteria to treat illnesses. And fight other bacteria and viruses. . . .

There are already probiotic supplements now routinely prescribed after a course of antibiotics. There are specific probiotic supplements which, taken at the start of the spring season, appear to reduce significantly the onset of "hay fever". . . .

We are just scratching the surface. This may be one of the most exciting new areas of exploration in health care, with relatively low-cost and high-impact interventions.

Some bacteria in the human **microbiome,** we know to be beneficial to health. Others are perhaps harmful, especially if they move to a different part of the gut.

Some are symbiotic. Bacteria in our large intestines help produce and absorb Vitamin B12, without which we would not be able to produce blood.

Apparently we each have a unique bacterial "fingerprint", starting with what we inherit from our mothers, even from the process of childbirth (C-section or normal). These are then shaped throughout life by our lifestyle and food choices.

And we start to understand the intriguing links to health. C-section born babies are more susceptible to allergies. Bacteria from an obese mouse transplanted to a lean mouse apparently makes that animal obese.

A quick Google search reveals several companies and startups engaged in this space. Like 4D Pharma, Enterome, Vedanta Biosciences, Second Genome, etc.

According to a Nov '20 article in Nature.com, large pharma companies such as Merck, Gilead, Genentech and J&J have also made strong bets on microbiome startups in the last few years.

In general, however, among large Pharma majors there remains a certain sense of scepticism until large clinical trials can establish the efficacy of new treatment protocols using the microbiome, and point the way to commercial value generation.

3. AGEING AND THE WEARING OUT OF BODY PARTS OR ORGANS, OFTEN ACCELERATED BY LIFESTYLE OR DIET

There are, broadly, two directions – both very exciting in speed as well as potential impact on human health!!

A) Genetics

In recent years, we have seen our understanding of genetics, DNA, RNA, and the use of stem cells (with the potential to develop into any body cell) grow by leaps and bounds. Technology now allows us to sequence the genetics of the Covid virus, develop an RNA-based vaccine, and scale it across the globe within a short 12 months!! And costs of gene sequencing have crashed dramatically over the last two decades and are perhaps headed still lower.

Applications of this technology are seen across disciplines, from evolutionary biology to the application of genetics to areas as diverse as ancestry mapping and identifying disease markers for pharmaceutical drug design and discovery.

This is technology with a truly transformative impact on society and a potentially dangerous one in the hands of the unscrupulous.

At the relatively "easy to defend" level is the application of this technology to understand disease markers, identify treatments likely to be effective, and even suggest health care and lifestyle choices.

Pharmaceutical companies are rushing to acquire or create such databases that can help them shorten drug development lead-times as well as provide more targeted applications.

Personalised nutrition is another key trend tailored to an individuality genetics. The science of nutrigenomics is an exciting and emerging opportunity for food and beverage companies that can develop and offer personalised nutrition at scale.

However, the very power of this technology raises serious ethical issues. The development of CRISPR technology allows researchers to snip off and add genes. If the Covid virus was indeed lab created (as has been alleged by the Washington Post, the Guardian, and others), then possibly a technology like CRISPR was used.

What are the limits on the use of this technology? Is cloning ethical? We know it's technologically feasible. We also know that, while several international protocols prescribe voluntary limits on this technology, the genie is now out of the bottle, and there is little to stop an unscrupulous government from creating national gene maps, then using this technology to try and create "super humans". The idea has existed for quite some time and was even pursued (unsuccessfully at the time) by the Nazis!

The economic and enterprise opportunity for the application of an enhanced understanding of genetics to personalise nutrition and healthcare is compelling.

The Economist magazine published, in August 2021, a leader asking the question, **"what if everybody's nutrition was personalised"?**

They refer to a landmark study in 2015 by researchers at the Weizmann Institute in Israel, who devised an algorithm, using AI, that could accurately predict any individual's response to any specific food, by continuously measuring blood glucose response using sensors attached to the arm.

This study was quickly replicated by other scientists, and has spurred the development of a number of startups, each helping people make choices on what to eat, what to avoid, and what to stock at home. EatLogic, the second largest was reportedly acquired by Google.

We are familiar with "23&me", which focuses on European and American populations. Similarly startups like the Anuva, based at Singapore and also the Sanger Institute at Oxford are pioneering data collection for Indian and Asian populations.

Once sequenced, this data can be shared with one's medical practitioner to identify risks. Also this data can be piped over digitally to companies like DNAfit.com, who can analyse it and let one know susceptibility to various diseases…And even make dietary recommendations (such as "eat more nuts and seeds" or "avoid caffeine", etc).

The authors expect this economic opportunity to grow exponentially as more companies discover the power of this technology to enhance quality of life.

What will this area bring? Will nightmarish Frankensteins become the stuff of reality? As always, a tool (like fire) brings with it the possibility of great good and great evil. It is our societies that need to evolve to a greater understanding of our fundamental interdependency on this fragile planet.

B) Technology and the bionic man (woman)

It is now technologically feasible to design new body parts to replace worn-out body parts. Dental implants have long been commonplace. Eye lenses are now commonplace after cataract surgery, thereby allowing a debilitating disease to be controlled.

Similarly, hearing aids and hip and knee replacements are increasingly common. Advances in material sciences and design are ensuring that these replacements have "useful lives" of decades.

Similarly, there is now the possibility of developing organ replacements for even more crucial organs like the kidney or the heart. Several researchers are already working to improve this technology and bring it to market.

An article from Futurism.com published in December 2017, explores the question: **are we entering an era where transplants are obsolete?**

They observe that it is possible to use 3D printing to successfully re-create organs like the thyroid gland, tibia replacements (already used on patients), and even a patch of heart cells that actually beat. similarly, advances are being made on growing bio artificial kidneys.

These could well help address the issue of donor shortage and the illicit and illegal organ trading industry.

Add to this, we may add the potential of stem cell therapy for regeneration of body parts or cells, and we start to see many possibilities for a longer and better life – as well as a host of business opportunities.

There are already hospitals dedicated to cataract surgery or to hip and knee replacements. Stem cell centres in the Caribbean have become popular amongst ageing people in the US. . . . There are large, emerging opportunities for business to specialise and offer applications of these emerging technologies.

This will extend human life span and also add "life to years" by enabling people to stay active and productive well into their seventh or eighth decade of life. This will have profound implications for society and economies.

4. ACCIDENTS OR VIOLENCE CAUSED BY ANIMALS OR HUMANS

In "The Better Angels of our Nature" by Steven Pinker, he traces the evolution of violence through recorded history and observes that we have witnessed a steady decline in the rates of violence over the centuries, whether through war or crime. From the era of Genghis Khan whose Mongol warriors massacred "one in every nine" humans alive at the time, we have seen a steady decline of violent death. The 20th century, despite all the horrors of the two world wars, was the least violent century in human history. . . . Evidently, mankind has historically led lives that are short and prone to great violence!

He also notes that the current moments "feel" more unsafe and violent because of the ubiquity and instantaneous nature of media coverage for every act of violence or every accident, however remote the location.

Bombarded by this constant media stream, we believe we are living in dangerous times. The facts, however, speak to the exact opposite being the case, and a lot has been driven by improved systems of governance, democracy, and law and order.

Certainly, technology is an important accelerator here as well. The introduction of seat belts and air bags has reduced injuries and deaths in automobile crashes. Airline travel is even safer than in the past. The overprotective state (at times called the "nanny state") is very real. Gun control, cigarette bans, and other similar legislation seeks to improve life and safety.

Arguably, the "surveillance state", which monitors data (there are many who understandably, abhor this thought as an invasion of privacy and putting too much power in the hands of the government), may be able to prevent violent acts almost completely. The rise of security devices (another large and growing business) enables constant surveillance, using cameras to address crime but also health events (like falls by old people).

Paradoxically, we may be so successful at controlling accidental death or injury that we may inadvertently create a "risk aversion" in the general public. Interestingly, most adventurers in earlier generations took great risks at a time when the threat of a life curtailed by violence was all too real.

One wonders if many will sign up for Elon Musk's planned colonisation of Mars, with all the attendant risks, compared to an earthly existence that grows more comfortable and healthy by the day!!

5. THE "FIFTH HORSEMAN": NEW DISRUPTIVE HEALTH CARE BUSINESS MODELS

We will see the emergence of new and disruptive health care models which will lead the surge towards universal and affordable health care. There is a growing consciousness (spurred by Covid) of the importance of creating health care models that are available to economically weaker countries and populations as well. We see already that, in the absence of universally available and affordable vaccines, Covid-19 may well become an endemic and unwelcome addition to the list of pathogens humanity has to learn to live with.

Health care, and particularly preventive health care, is a priority for human development, with high pay-back in terms of diseases controlled and populations enabled to explore their full human potential.

> We see the corporatisation of health care, with the development of hospital chains, pharmacy chains, and new distribution models evolving to leverage the internet.
>
> One such fascinating **startup in Africa is mPharma,** which connects doctors, patients, pharmacies and caregivers to ensure supply of authentic drugs and monitor compliance.

Despite advances, over 30% of babies in South Asia and sub-Saharan Africa are still being born stunted, with low birth weight and height. Hopefully, this can be addressed within the next generation by using the power of the internet, access to better nutrition, and preventative medicine.

There are already several startups in the "not-for-profit" space, like "Rocket Learning" in India, which are trying to bring best-in-class learning and parenting techniques to underprivileged children below the age of five, in an attempt to reduce the learning and development gap before children enter formal schooling.

Today, telemedicine, as discussed previously, is helping address challenges of access, cost, and quality. We will doubtless see many new and disruptive business models in the space to create business and societal value.

At the same time, the trend towards corporatisation of health care will likely accelerate in the developing world. Countries and regions which offer quality health care at affordable costs may become "digital tourism magnets" for the world (see box).

> The Bumrungrad Hospital in Bangkok re-invented themselves during the 1998 ASEAN financial crisis, and created a business model that attracts patients from around the world in search of affordable quality. An entire ecosystem of hotels and resorts has emerged around this hub.
>
> Today, this hospital is registered with insurers in several developed countries. And they reported in 2019 an annual sales turnover of 18 billion Baht, or about 500 million US dollars.
>
> From one hospital!!
>
> To be sure, with Covid-19 and travel restrictions their 2020 revenues have fallen sharply, but the underlying model is sound and one many across the globe and particularly emerging markets, will seek to copy.

Pharma and insurance will, likewise, be disrupted. Already, since 2015, insurers like John Hancock and other insurance companies offer discounts if you allow 24/7 monitoring of your activity levels via a "connected" motion device like a Fitbit. If you are active, the premiums decline and they rise if you are inactive.

We can expect value migration in health care to newer sectors, led by multiplier technologies.

Similarly, holistic alternate medical systems, like Ayurveda or Chinese as well as Yoga are becoming more popular.

Disruptions across the health care sector, covering several aspects of health care, have the potential to not only transform our life and "add healthy years to our life", but also create huge opportunities for enterprise. And a healthier population will almost inevitably mean a more productive population and workforce with extended working lives. Leading to both economic growth and opportunities for enterprise.

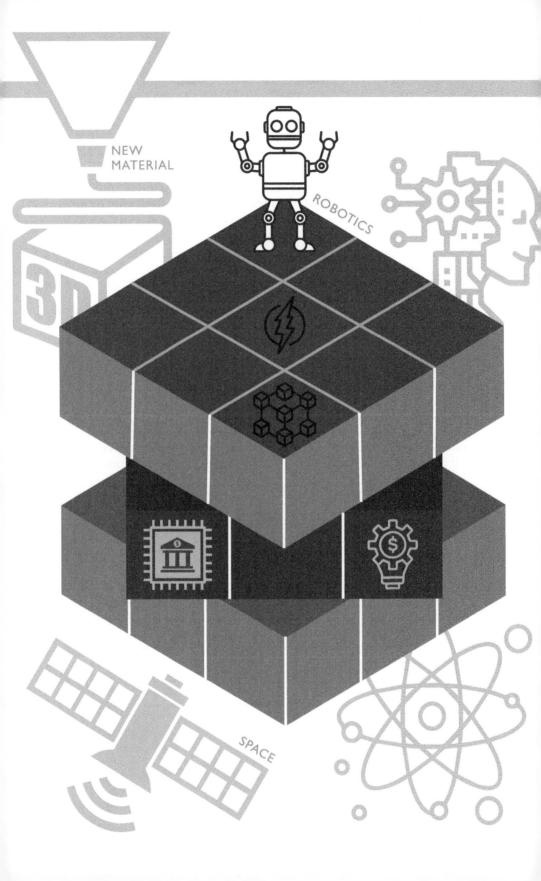

NEW
MATERIAL

ROBOTICS

SPACE

Chapter 11
Disruptions in the Power to Do
Future Revolutions

"It is difficult to make predictions, especially about the future"
– Mark Twain

We have looked so far at the disruptions arising out of several technologies like connectivity, health care, and other related areas. Many other significant technologies are emerging, and every day, we get glimpses of breakthroughs with powerful new possibilities.

What are the future disruptors on the horizon? What waves of change and opportunity will they unleash?

It's a wide and fascinating canvas and it is not possible for a book like this to be exhaustive in its coverage. However, we focus on a few key ones to help illustrate their power to change how people get things done. To understand the emerging forces of disruption and their implications for enterprise.

BACKGROUND

It was the late 1800s when three revolutionary, new technology applications dramatically and serendipitously came together as an outcome of the accelerating scientific advances triggered a century prior: electricity, telephone, and the internal combustion engine (the motor car).

These three technologies dominated and shaped the entire 20th century, affecting the business environment, politics, war, and even societal evolutions. Sadly, several villages in South Asia and Africa have not benefited from this fundamental accelerator and are still without electricity. However, they are becoming the exceptions rather than the rule, even in developing countries.

As we enter the 21st century, the rate of technological change is accelerating, as several technologies come together as "enablers or platforms" that trigger even more changes, often building on each other in a symbiotic manner.

We see several new and emerging, key technological platforms which will help shape the coming decades:

* **Blockchain and other foundational, enabling tech.**

DOI: 10.4324/9781003254737-13

- **Moore's law and the future of miniaturisation. Quantum technologies, disrupting communication and computing.**

- **Material sciences and nanotechnology. New materials, graphene structures.**

- **Particle physics.**

- **Energy storage and battery technology.**

- **Robotics.**

- **Space, satellites. And related technologies.**

- **3D printing.**

Indeed, these technologies will each have a "cascade" effect, with impact across several business sectors.

There are hundreds, if not thousands, of such changes headed our way. Each will cascade or build off the other. The future is likely to look very different, even as few as ten years from now.

"Space...the final frontier"...To "Trekkies" like the authors, this phrase by Gene Roddenberry fires our imagination.

We are enthused by the **diversification of human efforts** to develop technologies for space travel, which, in every case, should have effects that ripple back into industry and society.

From state-led efforts driven by NASA and Russia, newcomers like China and India have reduced the cost of putting satellites into space, while Elon Musk, Jeff Bezos and Richard Branson are bringing the private sector into this area, and innovating in models, material, and the application of technology. Space tourism. Mining of asteroids. Colonisation of other planets...the opportunities for enterprise are limitless.

Though it is difficult to try and predict exact disruptions – as Mark Twain famously observed, "it is difficult to make predictions, especially about the future" – we can create a framework to help guide our thinking about what they might be.

i) **Technologies that enable simplicity and convenience at the "last mile", close to the point of use or consumption.**

ii) **Enabling technologies that facilitate efficiency and sustainability at the back-end, out of sight of consumers, but nevertheless, revolutionary in their impact.**

iii) **"Platform technologies" that may trigger several other disruptions that build on them.**

We will examine each in turn:

1. TECHNOLOGIES THAT ENABLE SIMPLICITY AND CONVENIENCE AT THE "LAST MILE", CLOSE TO THE POINT OF USE OR CONSUMPTION

Self-driving cars are a great example of this, as we've discussed. So, too, are "connected" devices within your home.

3D printing, or "additive manufacturing", is another technology which promises to allow "last-mile personalisation" by enabling the "factory" to be located inside your own home. This is already being used extensively for fabricating parts out of plastic (see the following box).

3D printing, or additive manufacturing, is the construction of a three dimensional object from a computer aided and designed model. The term **"3D printing"** can refer to a variety of processes in which material is deposited, layer by layer, using plastics or other material, to create a composite object that corresponds to the design.

3D printing promises to revolutionise the development of medical prosthetics which are personalised. Artificial arms, legs, or even potentially other body parts…maybe even organs? There are several people working on these possibilities.

It probably won't be long before someone invents a 3D printer that prints tools, or fixtures as required to specifically suit the "factory or workplace" application using plastics or other materials that allow easy handling and deposition.

Coffee machines or food processing units are already being deployed inside homes. Emerging IoT technology will allow ovens or refrigerators to even communicate with humans.

Similarly, consider an oven which senses the food and, depending on the preparation required, chooses its own settings. (The startup "Innit" is a smart kitchen platform that uses AI to help you shop and cook nutritionally optimised food.)

It is not too difficult to imagine a futuristic kitchen which will prepare food and beverages, using fresh ingredients, ordered via e-commerce, and powered by artificial intelligence to even create healthy food menus. Or vegan food. Or gluten-free cuisine.

Similarly, e-commerce enabled auto-replenishment of pantries (see box).

The home and personal care company **Procter & Gamble** already pioneered a few years ago a **"Tide" button** on your washing machine. Whenever you are low on detergent, you just press the button and it triggers an order on e-commerce.

Or yet others are experimenting with refrigerators that sense when shelves are empty and automatically trigger orders to replenish themselves…

"Digital banking" is an idea whose time has come. Consumers are shifting to the convenience of banking over their mobile devices. Supporting and enabling technologies will bloom, while brick and mortar banking will inevitably decline.

In a similar manner, as we saw in the chapter on life sciences, **primary medical care** and diagnosis will also move into and reside in our personal digital assistants.

As will on-demand **concierge services,** and so on.

2. ENABLING TECHNOLOGIES THAT FACILITATE EFFICIENCY AND SUSTAINABILITY AT THE BACK-END, OUT OF SIGHT OF CONSUMERS, BUT NEVERTHELESS REVOLUTIONARY IN THEIR IMPACT

Renewable energy will power the world.

Renewable energy sources like hydroelectric, solar, wind, or tidal energy have come into their own recently and will develop even more in the future. It has been often observed that the Stone Age ended not because we ran out of stone, but because we discovered superior materials, like bronze and iron. Similarly, the age of oil might well be at an end as we discover alternative, non-polluting, renewable energy sources and are able to harness technology to substantially reduce their cost.

Generation of electricity close to the point of consumption will also lower distribution losses and reduce costs. Already, governments in several parts of the world subsidise rooftop solar power generation; "net metering", where you feed the grid during the day and use electricity off the grid at night, paying only for excess energy used, is already standard practice in several cities around the world.

This access to abundant, lower-cost energy will accelerate and spur development of applications that use electricity.

Tesla is known to be an electric car company with a market capitalisation greater than the other top car companies combined (as of this writing). The market evidently knows something about future prospects of this technology.

Governments around the world from the US to EU to China are crafting legislation to make electric vehicles more attractive and even (potentially) mandatory within the decade. To be fair, this is not without controversy, with some estimates claiming these EVs come with their own environmental challenges in disposal and recycling of batteries as well as mining of rare earths to support the technology.

One of the key concerns historically in **"green energy"** platforms like solar or wind is that they are not very predictable or stable in their output. When it's night, for instance, or on a day with less wind…one still needs a fallback source to supply energy.

Much effort has gone into developing better battery and energy storage technologies. This brings with it several challenges, such as "how to develop an industry standard" so that batteries can be interchangeable and recyclable.

Several startups are engaged in this exciting field, with promising new technologies under development.

Tesla are also pioneers in energy storage and battery technology with their "Powerwall", an energy storage unit that allows re-charging using unconventional and renewable sources like Solar. Indeed, several analysts believe this is their key competitive technology, even more than self-driving cars…

Energy storage technology is an enabling tech that is advancing by leaps and bounds and is further feeding the development of renewable energy generation.

Environmental restoration:

As concern over climate change gathers momentum, a fundamental demand from Millennials is that we move our thinking away from environment conservation to **environment restoration**. Companies will increasingly be judged (and rewarded) by how well they perform on this metric.

We will see companies shift away from single-use plastics to recycled and recyclable materials and practices. Of course, inevitably, there will be attempts at "greenwashing", which will make headlines and be penalised by an erosion of stakeholder trust. But the trend is now unstoppable. Bioplastics, integrated recycling programs in the supply chain, will be a minimum price of participation in the new economy.

The "3 Rs" methodology – **"REDUCE, RE-USE, RECYCLE"** thinking – will become a standard part of how companies operate. Plastics is emerging as a major area of concern, with micro-plastics infiltrating our food chain. Companies like "Banyan Nation" in Hyderabad, India are leading efforts to recycle plastics by providing structure to the informal recycling (scavenger) economy.

Ocean clean-up programs are already underway and will gather steam, with greater awareness of the fragility and interconnectedness of our ecosystem.

Robotics is a fundamental enabling technology which is already re-doing factories and factory jobs all over the world.

Robots rarely make mistakes, don't take downtime, or go on strike. Low capital costs encourage investment in robotics and we will see increasing adoption.

Initially, most robots are very specialised at doing specific, repetitive tasks. As more general-purpose robots are developed that can perform a variety of functions and even learn now jobs, this limited role will expand.

Similarly in offices, we see **software bots** redoing the nature of office work. Anything that can be defined as a set of rules and sent down a wire to an outsourcing centre can be done equally well by a software bot. Already today, in many industries, this impact is felt. Paralegals are seeing work dry up as the process of "discovery" is more efficiently performed by software bots.

3. "PLATFORM TECHNOLOGIES" THAT MAY TRIGGER SEVERAL OTHER DISRUPTIONS THAT BUILD OFF THEM

We see several new, emerging technology building-blocks that may serve as **platforms** to spur innovation. The development of "cloud-based" storage and computing services was one such "platform" which fostered innovation over the last decade.

In an earlier chapter, we have discussed implications for health care of **genetics** and lowered costs of gene sequencing creating greater access to better and newer health care technologies.

The development of **artificial intelligence** is another such technology which we discussed previously.

Even the way we look at water is changing with **creative use of technology.**

It has been forecast that one of the scarce commodities of the 21st century will be water, with the possibility of wars being fought over access to water resources.

Entrepreneurs have come up with unique ideas to harness and conserve this scare resource.

Singapore has led the way by converting the Singapore River (a saline creek inlet from the sea) to a fresh water storage at sea level. The concept is very simple. Build a dam at the mouth of the river or inlet. Allow tidal forces to pull out saline water at low tide, and at high tide block the dam, and allow rainwater from tropical storms to fill up the reservoir.

In the process, a few weeks are all it takes to convert the salinity of the water, thereby storing fresh water "inside the sea".

In a similar vein, Singapore has led the way by recycling water. Called NeWater, this is recycled, potable water supplied to all new developments in the city.

Israel have also pioneered the use of technology in water conservation and use, to become a water surplus nation in an otherwise arid location.

We will see similar and more creative ideas being adopted all over the world as we harness technology to support and take advantage of natural processes to improve fresh water storage and availability.

Entrepreneurs in India are reviving traditional water harvesting and storage systems to alleviate water stress…factories proudly share how they are water neutral.

Water conservation and recycling promise to be an exciting new opportunity for enterprise.

Blockchain is an enabling technology that may have transformative impact on several sectors, including banking, information storage, and sharing.

Initial applications of this technology have been to create digital crypto currencies that exist outside control of any government central banks.

These have been inherently unstable stores of value so far but have also been tools of speculation which have created windfall fortunes.

It is possible that "officially supported" digital

To quote from the website **"Blockchain Council"**, "Blockchain is a peer-to-peer decentralised distributed ledger technology that makes the records of any digital asset transparent and unchangeable and works without involving any third-party intermediary.

It is an emerging and revolutionary technology that is attracting a lot of public attention due to its capability to reduce risks and frauds in a scalable manner."

This technology has immense applications in enabling real-time, seamless financial transactions, or communications over the supply chain, has the power to render the "middleman" redundant, because people and enterprises will be able to collaborate with each other, directly.

This opens up immense opportunities for enterprise as **"tech savvy" startups** create novel means to create supply chain transparency, or even seamless currencies will be launched, legitimising these efforts. China was one of the first, launching, in 2021, a "digital yuan".

Larger applications of this technology may involve supply chains, helping create (incorruptible) ledgers for information monitoring and sharing, leading to more efficiency and transparency in the system. It may also be used for any form of confidential, yet protected information sharing between two individuals. Various applications of this underlying technology will probably emerge with time.

Indeed, while listing these technologies and the resulting changes, we are all too aware that we cannot be exhaustive in defining such a list. Space exploration creates new tech; new materials like graphene are emerging; new energy generation tech could be transformational. Each could be a platform for further disruptive technologies.

We welcome reader comments to help build this reference inventory of transformative technologies over time and look forward, to finding an appropriate and creative solution to providing an open-source access to add such developments.

Chapter 12
A World of Change
Perspectives for Business

In this epoch of disruption, a few key questions emerge. How is the world of the consumer transforming? How should enterprise view these shifts, and how can they best take advantage of them? What pivotal beliefs can guide us as we sail towards the emerging era?

Powerful forces are shaping us today. In previous chapters, we have looked, individually, at the disruptions and their impact. Here, instead, we step back and take a holistic look at our **world of change**. A world where **consumer lives are being transformed**, and a host of possibilities are being unleashed **for enterprise to seize**.

We explore the four critical perspectives that will influence the choices and success of enterprise as it performs in this crucible of change.

a. **The facets of disruptive change and the opportunities they represent.**

b. **Pivotal beliefs that impact how enterprise engages with change.**

c. **A new world – the big shifts in consumer lives and society.**

d. **From sensing the change to seizing the opportunity – the imperative of action.**

I. THE FACETS AND OPPORTUNITIES OF CHANGE

A) The forces of disruptive change

We live in an epoch of disruption. Powerful pivots of change are breaking through:

- Some are driven by scientific knowledge – technological pivots changing the way we do things – e.g., AI – which add human like intelligence to actions or social networks, which change the way people interact.

- Others are big societal shifts about who we are – our demographics, socio-economics, our beliefs, and even our changing institutions.

DOI: 10.4324/9781003254737-14

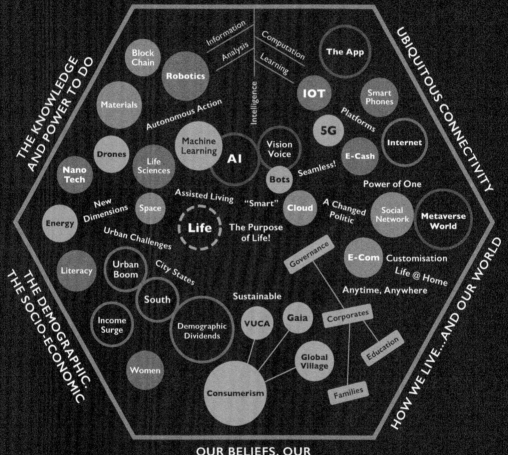

INTELLIGENCE ADDED

THE KNOWLEDGE AND POWER TO DO

UBIQUITOUS CONNECTIVITY

Information

Computation

Analysis

Learning

The App

Block Chain

Robotics

IOT

Smart Phones

Materials

Intelligence

Platforms

Autonomous Action

5G

Internet

Drones

Machine Learning

Vision Voice

E-Cash

Nano Tech

Life Sciences

AI

Bots

Seamless!

Power of One

Assisted Living

"Smart"

Cloud

A Changed Politic

Social Network

Metaverse World

New Dimensions

Space

Energy

Life

The Purpose of Life!

E-Com

Customisation

Urban Challenges

Governance

Life @ Home

Literacy

Urban Boom

City States

Anytime, Anywhere

Income Surge

South

Sustainable

VUCA

Gaia

Corporates

Demographic Dividends

Education

Women

Global Village

Consumerism

Families

HOW WE LIVE...AND OUR WORLD

THE DEMOGRAPHIC. THE SOCIO-ECONOMIC

OUR BELIEFS. OUR SOCIETAL INSTITUTIONS

- Often, a new, nodal reality coalesces that itself becomes a force for change. For example, an outcome of the digital transformations, "anytime anywhere living" is a new paradigm for living that is shaping our world.

These forces are dynamic and evolving. They interact and combine, often fusing with great transformative power. It is a bubbling cauldron of change (see, along with a visual representation, a cartography of some of the salient forces of change). We believe that understanding the pivots and envisioning their impact by using tools like "thought experiments" can reveal new possibilities. And creatively re-imagining a new reality, using the pivots and domain insights, can help us unlock big, new opportunities.[1]

B) The two "opportunities of change"

Our society has transformed. The world is increasingly urbanised, and the economic universe has had a "big bang" expansion with the inclusion of emerging economies. We have a different demographic, and a different mind-set drives us.

This **change is an opportunity in itself**; enterprise can identify and better address the needs of a world that is changing.

Further, a surge of powerful technologies is amplifying these emerging changes. Our notion of the "space and time" in which we live, work, or play is changing. With ubiquitous connectivity, our actions today are migrating to an anytime-anywhere world. We are mirroring our lives to seamlessly live parallel lives in a metaverse. And intelligence, once only a human prerogative, can now potentially be added to multiply the value in every action and transaction, creating previously unimagined possibilities.

Digital transformation drives new technologies in every field and even in the creation of new knowledge itself. New technologies are emerging in domains like health care and materials, with potential to power further waves of change.

Indeed, **"to drive change" is the second opportunity** – an opportunity in itself to develop new technologies, to re-imagine the way we live, and drive the change we want to see.

C) The change will become more pervasive; the impact, much more disruptive

- We already sense the impact of the forces of change today in everyday life. Digital technologies drive our world of change. Their impact, while dramatic, is still limited by the current access to the digital world. Take the example of smart phones – the engines of digital transformation in the consumer world. Despite their impressive impact, they are used by only a fraction of the world's population. As costs plummet, adoption will increase. Potentially, everyone in the world will enjoy digital access and the impact will increase dramatically.

- For all the proven benefits of these technologies, there is a lot left lying on the table. The advantages of digital initiatives like connectivity, apps, e-commerce, and cloud computing are well accepted, but a dominant majority of businesses don't yet leverage the full benefits.

As technologies prove their impact, innovative new-use cases pop up in existing spaces, and applications extend into new domains. For example, we are witnessing a surge in AI applications disrupting fields as varied as smart homes, defence models, or weather forecasting. IoT applications are just beginning to enter consumer homes and industries, but hold the promise to transform households and enterprise alike.

In the words of William Gibson, an American-Canadian writer, "The future is already here. It's just unevenly distributed". There is a lot still to be gained by **adopting and cross-fertilising existing best practices**.

- Yes, technologies that make the world more efficient are delivering big benefits. But truly disruptive impact has been driven by re-inventing our world. Social media, artificial intelligence, and drones have added new dimensions to our world.

New technologies are emerging that can create new paradigms, processes, and industries (going beyond just improving current ones); can transform lives.

Powerful next generational technologies, like 5G and beyond, not only strengthen the existing connectivity benefits but promise to open up new "beyond the horizon" possibilities, like driverless cars and other low-latency applications. Advances in domains like life sciences, robotics, and space show the promise to re-invent our world once again.

D) A kaleidoscope of change: technologies coalesce to multiply disruption

Diverse advances are coming together to create powerful new realities. For example, voice recognition, connectivity, IoT, and cloud applications are combining with artificial intelligence to transform homes into smart homes with virtual assistants. And in health care, material science, nanotechnology, and AI are bringing about the next generation of health tech devices.

Often, there is a **hop, step, and jump of disruption**; connectivity and computational technologies have powered the development of fintech-based payment systems. And that, in turn, has not merely altered how transactions can be paid for, but has fundamentally transformed market structures with the growth of online commerce. Equally – a spin-off – direct-benefit transfers and digital banking are significantly advancing social impact and financial inclusion for societies at the "bottom of the pyramid".

Truly disruptive initiatives have far-reaching effects. Powerful technological benefits can transform the way consumers live. Often, a new paradigm of living forms multiplies the disruption. Witness the growth of social media technologies and businesses. They have enabled individuals to express themselves and connect with a wide audience, driving action and influencing change. The "power of one" that this has released is perhaps one of our most fundamental shifts. It has further gone to transform our societal relations, our media, and indeed, the very body politic of the world.

Connected networks are another platform for exponential increases in disruption. Twitter gets its impact from its pervasiveness. As networks grow larger, the wave spreads to gather even more disruptive energy, unlike real-life tsunamis, which attenuate as they spread.

Perhaps the most powerful multiplier is emerging: the ability of artificial intelligence and machine learning can help build new knowledge in domains where the human mind could not reach. A multiplication of technologies by technology.

The foregoing are but a few examples of how technological forces interact to deliver a kaleidoscope of benefits. Envisioning new realities by creatively using technology developments can exponentially multiply their impact.

2. PIVOTAL BELIEFS ON HOW THE CHANGE CAN IMPACT ENTERPRISE

A) Disruption will help us do better, be better

The transformational changes we are seeing have the potential to make the world better. The power to improve productivity, make our economy more efficient, to generate surpluses that are the foundation of well-being. As we have seen in earlier chapters, technologies provide solutions where none existed earlier – for saving lives, for solving our sustainability issues, and for enhancing the quality of human life.

Innovative companies help make the world better. And innovative organisations that have embraced the change have done better.

B) Embracing change for benefit is the opportunity for all

No industry is exempt – large or small, traditional or a trendsetter.

In a short period of time, we have seen unprecedented market shifts in even the largest of industries – those that are the bulwark of our economies. A case in point is the automobile industry. Long the archetypal backbone of growing economies, the industry has transformed in the short period of a decade. Today, chips are determining success as much as new engines. Electric vehicles are setting the mainstream agenda in the industry.

Technologies are re-shaping even seemingly conventional fields. Use of drone-based technologies is now, in India, a major thrust for agricultural development.

Even small traders, for example of traditional and casual jewellery, are finding an opportunity in online selling, tapping into the consumer preference of "anytime-anywhere" shopping.

Consumer expectations are changing, and that, in turn, is compelling industry to change to seize the opportunity.

Not only market opportunities – technology is capturing new efficiencies, and advantageously, reshaping business processes and models in almost every form of enterprise – in marketing and supply chain, in the world of venture financing, in the surge of "crowd sourcing". Here again, a benefit can be found in every process.

A strong reason for the probable universality of disruption by technology, digital transformation impacts levers that are the foundation of any individual or enterprise activity. "Connecting" to act (across the value chain or with consumers) is fundamental to every enterprise. And we have observed that information and intelligence shape every human or business action. Hence, as disruptions happen in this foundation of how we can connect or how intelligence can get added to tasks, every process has the potential to change; every industry can transform.

We could even consider something to be really amiss, if a big change opportunity were "not" being seen. In fact, if a business is not embracing relevant disruptions, it is likely to falter.

The opportunities of disruptive change extend to a wide variety of people:[2] active investors, technologists, entrepreneurs, governments, law makers, social scientists, and academics and more. (Witness the rapid adoption of social media by political parties!)

C) People first!

The disruption opportunity is about making a positive difference in people's lives. This is not to reduce the importance of technology as an enabler; rather, to emphasise the primacy of the impact on consumer lives.

Really disruptive technology transforms a fundamental consumer reality. Understanding this helps us drive more, and better, change. For example, in a world without mobile phones, unconnected consumers cannot as easily take productive actions together. Connectivity enables access and actions – it makes fallow moments productive. Mobile apps, e-commerce sites, or social media all build on this "transformation by connectivity" to re-imagine our world.

Disruption happens only when a consumer adopts a product. Often, technologies have existed for a long time but products have explosively grown only after removing barriers to effortless human adoption. A lot of the technologies behind marketplaces and other online applications have existed for a long time. However, it is the affordable and handy access with the arrival of smart phones that has triggered explosive growth.

Astute companies remain focussed on the ultimate consumer benefit or value. A health app is not an app business. It is a health business delivering invaluable health benefits via an app as a tool. This represents a small, nuanced shift in articulation but an enormous shift to a value perspective.

The opportunity is about connecting path-breaking technology with a deep customer insight to disruptively deliver a valued consumer benefit.

D) Transformational shifts and societal issues

New, associated issues will arise related to the social, political, or economic impact of technological disruption. For example, questions about ethics and privacy are emerging today with the omnipresence of social media. Surfacing and resolving such issues are an inherent part of the transformational journey.

3. THE BIG SHIFTS IN CONSUMERS' LIVES AND SOCIETY

Big changes are happening in "who we are" and "what we think". We have seen how new technologies are delivering disruptive, new benefits and changing the way we act. Collectively, they are changing how we live, what we consume, our needs, and our product expectations. And this, in turn, is changing the context in which the world of enterprise delivers on needs and markets.

We focus on the **power themes[3] that are redefining the key pivots of consumer lives.**

A NEW DEMOGRAPHIC   **A transformed underlying demographic; a new consumer life context**

- A life in our new mega urban habitats with a new societal profile is driven by tumult in age pyramids and nuclear family structures. Livelihoods that are not blue- or white-collar – perhaps best expressed as X-collar – with intelligence and the human value-addition becoming widespread.

- And an even bigger change in how everyone lives, as disruptive technologies re-imagine life.

A RE-DEFINITION OF LIFE SPACES   **Life extends beyond our classical physical world**

- Communities are us, connected beyond boundaries.

- Living in the metaverse. The virtual world is increasingly the new reality.

- Anytime, anywhere, seamlessly connected – our world is always with us!

WHAT IS LIVING ABOUT?   A new focus in life

- A shift to the discretionary – self-expression and individual choice. Driven by a growth in income, a surplus beyond the requirements for basics.

- A reducing primacy of livelihood. A strengthening of "living" and experiences.

- Longer life-expectancy and an extended active-life changes motivations and behaviour.

OUR MIND SPACE   The forces that drive us

- "Power of one" energised. Social media and connectivity have unleashed individual expression and action. Driving diversity of thoughts, choices, and social groups.

- The appeal of Gaia. A oneness with nature and our communities permeates life and actions.

THE NEW PRODUCT PARADIGMS   Our product expectations and relationships

- Hyper-personalisation: "me and my choice" drives the growth of customisation and segmentation.

- Anytime, anywhere, anything drives access to our products and actions.

- Experience the benefit in full – beyond products to service. Integration of engagement, shopping, fulfilment, and consumption.

- "Assisted living" is the new norm (in so many ways!). "Bots and robots" facilitate how we do things. Peer reviews and guidance help us shop. And AI provides invaluable, intelligent support.

- Ownership to access: a shift from owning to its use and experience. Growth of pay per use.

A changing consumption basket and changing marketplaces

Historically, categories like food and personal care had a significant share of individual consumption. But this is changing, and areas like leisure, shopping, financial products, life assist, and health are surging ahead to become a significantly larger part of what we consume.

A part of this shift can be explained by rising incomes (classically, income growth has led to growth of categories beyond the basics of food, hygiene, and housing). But the big change today is being driven by the disruptive, new benefits enabled by new technologies.

More than just an increased size of industry, big shifts are happening in how benefits are being delivered and new benefits are emerging. A significant part extends beyond the growth of new products in existing categories to disruptions with the emergence of sizeable new categories – e.g., over-the-top (OTT) media services offered directly to viewers via the internet, online education, etc – and the spread from products to services – e.g., the rise of food service and deliveries versus packaged food. We are also starting to see products that reside only in the virtual world of the metaverse. E-greeting cards were its simplest form. Digital avatars, digital signatures, and the recent surge in value of non-fungible tokens (NFTs) are different expressions of this shift.

Value spaces and marketplaces of today – the playgrounds of enterprise – are rapidly changing.

Every domain of human activity is transforming

We see fundamental shifts; our consumers today live differently. We have, in previous chapters, already seen the big shifts in our life-spaces, like education, in the way we shop, and even in our institutions and governance.

Big forces are transforming the fundamentals of work: connectivity and remote working, the rise of independent work and the gig economy, and the restructuring of work itself with the growing impact of artificial intelligence.

We illustrate the big shifts in how we work and how we play (see box). Notice that these shifts are very tangible and have happened on scale, in a relatively short period of time. Similarly, technology and consumer shifts are transforming every industry.

THE SURGING WORLD, AND TRANSFORMATION OF LEISURE

Significantly larger. A structured and corporatized industry

- The growth of gaming, leagues, music, entertainment etc. Today one of the largest value spaces.

- A diversification e.g. the growth of mass evangelism (religion), spectator sports and sex (nudity and porn as a key driver of internet traffic, as the topic gets less taboo)

- An international diversity - the growing impact of Bollywood and K-dramas. The Korean BTS boy band received in the White House!

A growth of individualisation

- The revolution of the individual artist with free access to markets, without middlemen or brokers. YouTube. Music. Crypto based NFT to monetise artists' work.

- Ultra segmentation of niches. So every creative pursuit has traction when aggregated at a global scale

- Connectivity drives individualised delivery across income strata

The new worlds of leisure

- The rise of gaming with its own rules, universes, currencies

- Facebook, Google, Apple and Microsoft rushing to create interfaces and competing universes.

Successful businesses are not only sensitive to the shifts in their domain of business; they actively drive the change that the consumer would like to see.

We believe tapping the changes in consumers, their consumption, and life-spaces is the biggest single driver of success in the emerging era. An imperative for enterprise to insightfully understand and purposefully address the new opportunities in products and markets.

HOW WE "WORK" – A FEW SALIENT SHIFTS

The rise of individual enterprise

- People use individual assets to compete with large corporations e.g. AirBnB. Uber. Feastly.

- Revolution of the startup itchers. People everywhere emboldened by capital and tech to do their own.

- The revolution of the freelancers. Gig workers.

Connected working

- The revolution of the "work from home" addicts. Many prefer to live in a low cost location, often with parents, and do work remotely.

- The disaggregation of industry and increasing collaboration to deliver to the consumer. Globally.

The churn in organisations

- The rise of NGO/not-for-profit organisations focused on ESG causes. Social causes.

- The corporatisation of agriculture. Farmer producer organisations.

---

4. THE IMPERATIVE OF ACTION

We live in exciting times. We see, with increasing clarity, the forces of disruption re-imagining our world and throwing up opportunities, as societies embrace change like never before.

But for leaders of enterprise, we have to move beyond merely sensing the change, towards finding ways to seize the opportunity.

"The key to success isn't just thinking what we are doing but doing something about what we are thinking", writes Peter Senge.

The do-ability and advantages of seizing change opportunities are well established; we see inspiring examples of success all around us.

The Covid crisis has forcefully demonstrated, to the entire world, the latent power of disruptive technologies to transform people, enterprise, livelihoods, and governments alike.

But, as change makers and leaders of business, are we focussed on identifying and securing the opportunity with the emphasis it deserves?

THE COVID CRISIS WAS A "PEARL HARBOR MOMENT"

A period where a global crisis forced the world to actively embrace change.

It was a trigger to transform critical areas like work, health care and everyday consumption.

Things in daily lives we never imagined would change, shifted with unprecedented rapidity. To a profoundly **more digital and virtual life** that provided an effective solution to societal challenges of a severe global epidemic.

It brought out the latent benefit of technologies. And that with an action mantra, big shifts can be secured, rapidly, not just in the fringes, but in the mainstream of our society.

An urgent imperative to act exists.

The starting point for this is "a conviction" about the opportunity in the change, followed by purposeful action to seize the opportunity.

Enterprise is about thinking of new ideas and activities in business and making them successful, despite the risks involved. How do we build on our insights to harvest our opportunities? What can help us execute and navigate our success? In the next section, we focus on the issues, tools, and mindset required to seize this change opportunity – our action mantras for success in the new era.

"Following the light of the sun, we left the Old World"
– Christopher Columbus

NOTES

1 Part III of the book focusses on inspiring examples and application of these tools to discover our opportunities.
2 With our book's focus, it is natural that we have primarily showcased opportunities for people associated with the world of enterprise, commerce, and technology. However, the shifts are not merely technological or commercial in nature. In fact, the tumult and primary energies of disruption are deeply connected with human lives, society, and its institutions.

   Hence, we would like to emphasise that the changes are impacting, and profoundly so, every section of society, every profession. In particular, we would like to call out the high relevance of understanding the transformations to social scientists and academics. An opportunity to build a world of vital research and knowledge about the emerging era.
3 These themes are drawn from an understanding of the change drivers in earlier sections and tabulated here for a quick glance. They are a critical influence on business actions in our world of change.

Part III

The Action Mantras
Seizing the Opportunity

In the previous chapters, we've discussed at length the current maelstrom of change. We perceive the convergence of two powerful tsunamis of change:

- *The socioeconomic, demographic, and the digital transformation of our world described in Part I.*

- *The new disruptors on the horizon in the form of technologies in health care, material, or even the new genre of "knowledge technologies" discussed in Part II.*

These tsunamis amplify and build off each other to create a mega-tsunami, and every aspect of our lives is being re-imagined as our societies embrace change.

How do we delight them with disruptive possibilities? That is the focus of this section.

We start by declaring our stance.

We believe in this epochal opportunity. As the dance of disruption and creation opens up new possibilities, it is up to us to identify and "grab" the opportunity.

We believe in action: "Want to be the change you wish to see". And ACT to make the new future happen!

Three action mantras to harness the pivots of change. We examine each in a subsequent chapter.

1. **Re-imagine "value spaces".**

    Disruption is about changing lives, and changing lives changes markets. We start by recommending we **re-define, re-imagine and re-discover** markets as they morph. Build on the underlying changes and connect these with new technological possibilities to uncover new consumer truths, and define the new consumer paradigm.

    Re-imagine our market connection, product or service; the conventional organisation has to shed its skin and re-imagine what it could be to create a completely new, proprietary, and unique business paradigm.

DOI: 10.4324/9781003254737-15

2.   **Re-imagine enterprise**.

A special focus. How do we seek and use new technologies to re-imagine the way we uniquely deliver benefits or deliver new benefits. This includes developing new business models and new business assets (like data and customer relationships) which will underpin these new models.

How do we re-structure our business processes where, while the underlying principles remain the same, they have a business-transforming power when we leverage the new life-context and technologies to create competitive edge

3.   **Re-imagine organising**.

Having discovered our path is just the start. We need to manage the inherent tensions in navigating large, complex changes. How to drive your car while you change tires. How to choose the correct path. How to build talent that can manage today's processes efficiently while imagining new possibilities. Specifically, how do these apply to startups and beanstalks, as distinct from large companies?

A total re-imagination of our organisation and capabilities, starting with our mind-sets, very similar to the re-imagination of marketplace.

Chapter 13

Re-imagine Value Spaces

Challenge, Re-imagine, Imagine Anew

"Imagination is more important than knowledge. For knowledge is limited to all we now know and understand, while imagination embraces the entire universe, and all there ever will be to know and understand".

– Einstein

In previous sections, we have seen two powerful streams of disruptive change: the societal and the tech-led. They build off each other as they unfold to create a mega-tsunami and spur discontinuities headed our way from several directions.

Now, we look at harvesting the disruption with two starting points: a "market inspired" and a "technology inspired" one. These are two sides of the same coin, both seeking to identify and deliver highly appealing benefits, and are covered in two successive chapters. (There is some inevitable overlap because they each impact the other.)

In this chapter, as we take a market-inspired focus, we see consumer needs and benefits being fundamentally re-defined by the underlying evolution in demographics, societies, and economies. Simultaneously, amplified by tech, new benefit vectors are emerging, shaping consumer expectations, and enabling new possibilities.

We will share several examples and cases to inspire us to "re-imagine the value space" that we operate in. And challenge us to grab the opportunity and set up our enterprise for greater success. Ultimately, markets (which are an aggregation of products and benefits) will need to be re-imagined. Enterprises seize the opportunity of disruption through their essential core: benefits, products, markets, and how to deliver benefits for maximum impact.

We use a simple, two-pronged approach to discover our opportunities:

- First, **we mine the mother lodes of disruption** to identify and seize the big opportunities that have been uncovered in areas like sustainability, urbanisation, and demographic shifts.

- And, as a twin track, we emphasise **re-imagining value spaces to uncover new opportunities**. Amplified by tech, new benefit vectors are emerging, as the moment of consumption moves to "anytime, anywhere". We focus on discovering untapped niches, challenge the underlying assumptions,

DOI: 10.4324/9781003254737-16

re-imagine products to re-define consumer paradigms, and imagine fresh consumer paradigms to create new value spaces.

The next chapter will focus on the tech-led opportunities created by disruption, which enable new, highly appealing benefits. This will inevitably require changes in underlying business processes as well, which we will also discuss there.

To some extent, this is an artificial separation between "market led" change and "tech led" change because they each impact the other. The separation is only for ease of analysis and understanding. As we will see across Chapters 13 and 14, many areas will, inevitably, overlap because it is, in fact, like looking at two sides of the same coin.

The concepts we discuss here are relevant and can be applied whether one is in a large corporation or a startup. In government or in the armed forces. Or in an NGO. The size and field of operation doesn't matter.

There is a mega-tsunami of change coming, accompanied by a new music of disruption.

And one has to learn how to dance.

We will highlight the two aforementioned themes in discussion that follows. Within each theme, rather than suggest specific actions (which, by definition, can constrain you in a world of unconstrained change) on what specific steps each organisation should take, we will try and keep it simple.

We seek, instead, to **inspire the reader** to re-think business models by highlighting several success stories in each area.

I. MINE THE MOTHER LODES OF DISRUPTION TO RE-IMAGINE VALUE SPACES

An "outside-in" mindset is a good starting point. We should look at the changes happening around us and ask, "How could we make this work for us", rather than an "inside-out" approach where one looks at existing models and then reacts in response to changes.

In other words, start by looking widely at the market and society to **"discover the disruption"**.

Then formulate a strategic response.

In other words, pick any disruption and "embrace it" to be more proactive and aggressive, by asking,

> **"How could we drive this discontinuity and disruption created by this market shift to make it work for us by 'tweaking' our current models or by completely reimagining them?"**

Here are a few starting thoughts to highlight some opportunities:

Several opportunities exist at the "bottom of the pyramid" (BOP). Or are created by the "graying" of society and emergence of inverted demographic pyramids. The rising tide of urbanisation, combined with the transformation of established institutions, also yield fresh areas for companies to capitalise on. Re-imagined with technology to morph products and service, these opportunities will be sizeable. Each will require experimentation to figure out the best way to adapt one's business to tap into this opportunity.

> Here are some tools to help us shape our response to this **new mega-tsunami,** this **dance of disruption.** The tools, though somewhat generic in nature, are applicable across a variety of situations. It is the mindset with which we apply them that is critical.
>
> 1. Do thought experiments where we break all current rules.
>
> 2. Do small, controlled pilots to validate what tweaks to current models would serve this particular opportunity better.
>
> 3. Keep a watch on other startups which may have hit upon a successful model but are struggling to scale. Then see if any elements of their business model could apply to one: Invest in them or buy them.

We will highlight the four specific opportunities (that stand out to the authors) to "**discover the disruption**":

A) The bottom of the pyramid (BOP)

Large segments of society at the "bottom of the pyramid", especially across "emerging economies" in Africa and even parts of South Asia, begin to get enough affluence to actively participate in the global economy and (with dreams and aspirations inspired by access to mass media) gain access to modern goods and services. Companies which focus on this segment will continue to have a large market, across all geographies, but particularly those in Asia, Africa, and Latin America.

As C.K Prahlad observed in his famous book *The Fortune at the Bottom of the Pyramid*, there is a huge, latent demand for goods and services at the bottom of the pyramid.

Whether in the slums of Mumbai, Sao Paolo, or Manila, the poor often can't afford to purchase more than "single use" portions of products, and as a result, often end up paying more (on a per unit, per kg, or per litre basis) for what they consume!

A few examples:

- Payment services like **MPesa** in Kenya to empower small businessmen and consumers at the BOP.

- Pre-paid data packages for telephony at the BOP which allow these consumers to enter the world of anytime connectivity.

- Governance services and data stacks like the **Jan Dhan** and basic health care insurance launched by the government of India. Combined with the

Aadhar card and the **Unified Payments Interface** (UPI), this also enables direct bank transfers to people in need. The Economist Magazine of May 2022 estimates that as much as US$280 billion may have been transferred directly (and without leakages) in India to 950 million people over the last three years!

- The "sachet" format of consumer brands (think shampoo, coffee, or other foods).

- Farmer apps which allow the "Uberisation of tractors and equipment", or "market apps" which enable access to determine market prices for agricultural commodities.

Companies should look at these emerging opportunities and re-design their product/service as well as the entire value chain to cater to the specific needs at the BOP. It is important to use distribution channels that they have access to (and, luckily, consumers at the BOP are often early to embrace digital technology).

It would be good to also look at and benchmark the playbook used by Unilever, Nestle, Colgate, Vodafone, and others to access these markets so far in Asia and Africa. First-mover advantage is important, for this segment tends to be quite brand loyal.

B) Demographic shifts and opportunities

There are large, new emerging opportunities created by ageing societies:

- "Community retirement homes", for example. With Baby Boomers now retiring, the segment of senior citizens is one of the fastest growing demographics across societies. To avoid being a burden on their families, many seniors are voluntarily planning and moving into retirement homes with friends, in order to create a support system and community.

- "Pension plans" across the world (the earlier "defined benefit" plans created large, unfunded liabilities as people's life expectancy grew) have been re-designed as sustainable "defined contribution" (or equivalent savings and investment) plans to provide reasonable standards of living as one ages.

- "Health care plans" are being re-designed to cater to every budget and represent a fast-growing market, whether one is in the US or in India.

- "Medical care" for the elderly: gerontology and "diseases of the ageing" will grow to become a sizeable opportunity for medicine. New diseases like sarcopenia as well as existing ones like Alzheimer's will represent growing treatment fields, especially with rapidly ageing societies, like Japan.

- Pet ownership and pet care. Often, a root cause of many non-communicable diseases tends to be loneliness, which, in turn, leads to lower levels of exercise or appetite. Pets can be important providers of companionship as one ages, and therefore, we will probably see increased ownership of pets, like dogs or cats.

- There are several startups who are experimenting with business models to cater to this opportunity. We can, of course, benchmark (or acquire) these startups.

- But also important is to question how our products or services can be re-designed to cater to this large, emerging segment. Even simple innovations like making the fine print with nutrition labelling (or ingredients) on packaging larger and easier to read can be a significant differentiator. Additionally, ageing people often have developed allergies or sensitivities to certain ingredients.

In addition, Millennials are creating new opportunities. This emerging group of consumers, who are digital natives, care deeply about sustainability (see point "D"), bringing with them truly global attitudes and concerns.

- The growing concern for vegan food is a classic example. Or organic food. Local products. Artisanal products. The anti-"big food" movement is led by this generation, which distrusts large companies (whose profit motive they hold responsible for many of the world's ills).

- The emergence of global tribes and cross-cultural fusion, which has led to Indian food becoming the preferred cuisine in the UK, or Chinese food (with Indian spices) becoming a dominant "out of home" food preference in India, is another example of this growing "global" mindset.

Again, how can we re-design our offerings to cater to this emerging segment? Can we re-formulate with local (in-season) ingredients, highlight the (reduced) carbon footprint, or even invest in a reverse logistics chain to collect and recycle packaging? Can we launch vegan alternatives? The specific answers will vary and depend on the specific competitive advantages we can build into each business model.

C) Urbanisation as a key driver of new service-led opportunities

As urban agglomerations grow (Greater Delhi is expected to be the largest urban cluster in the world by 2030), they bring several new opportunities for enterprise. Here are a few illustrative ones:

- Last-mile delivery services like "**Shadowfax**" in India.

- Food delivery services like **Food Panda, Uber Eats, Swiggy, or Zomato**.

- Small grocery store suppliers and aggregators like **City Mall, Apna Klub, or Reliance Jio Mart** in India.

- Urban service aggregators like '**Urban Clap**', again in Delhi, which offer electricians, plumbers, or carpenters to address domestic needs.

This is an important opportunity for companies because there is a large, concentrated market for goods and services. Rather than diffuse one's efforts by going wide, can one focus on these large, urban agglomerations? Normally, millennials as well as ageing people tend to congregate in urban areas because of the facilities and convenience they provide.

D) Sustainability as an opportunity

The mainstreaming of Gaia, led by Millennials, will create new opportunities for products and benefits (whether tangible or perceived). We will list a few examples to inspire us to re-think, such as:

- Local supply chains. People will look for products grown locally, rather than imported from across the world.

- The carbon footprint of businesses and products will be scrutinised. Airlines already offer customers the option to buy carbon offsets.

- The "Reduce, Reuse, Recycle" mindset is one which many enterprises are looking at, in order to reduce their long-term environmental impact. Reduce waste, reuse technical materials, and recycle organic materials. In Chapter 14, we will look at emerging new business concepts that address these concerns.

- Traceable supply chains and reverse logistics chains are evolving to enable the retrieval of products to align with the "3R" philosophy mentioned previously.

- In a similar vein, companies can move to take virtual ownership of product use across the value chain (even after they have sold a product) by moving to a "product as a service" model. BMW has already announced plans for a car factory that can retrieve and reprocess cars after just a few years of use. Can we offer or design similar models? More in Chapter 14.

- Delivery can be a competitive advantage. Take beer, for example. One of the key costs of the supply chain is transporting large volumes of liquid across geographies. "Sustainable Beverage Technologies" in Denver is one such company seeking to create a greener beer. They have created a "non-alcoholic beer concentrate" that preserves flavour, can be transported easily, and can be reconstituted into beer closer to the point of consumption by adding back the desired alcohol levels and water. And without any compromise on taste.

  In fact, their non-alcoholic beer[1] has (surprisingly) won several awards for taste, even while competing with alcoholic beers!! (See link in chapter notes below.)

The concept of last-mile assembly that is used in this example may be a way forward for several products. Customisation close to the point of sale reduces environmental impact while preserving and even amplifying taste and flavour. After all, fresh food does taste better!!

Each of these examples should serve to inspire a re-think of business models and value chains. "Sustainability is the new Digital", says the World Economic Forum (WEF), and we are inclined to agree. Companies who are first movers will seize the advantage. We discuss more in Chapter 14 the concepts of sustainability and last-mile assembly.

There are many other such opportunities (mother lodes of disruption) beyond the four that we highlight. We invite the reader to discover these by mining each opportunity we describe in the previous two sections of this book. And by creating small experiments to learn how best to tweak business models to grab these opportunities.

2. RE-IMAGINE VALUE SPACES TO UNCOVER YOUR NEW OPPORTUNITIES

The key question to ask oneself is, "How could we reimagine business paradigms fundamentally, so that we become a 'monopoly' of one? A player with a unique product/brand/market offering. One that competition cannot (yet) copy".

We suggest four approaches to do this:

A) Discover untapped niches

Look for "niches" which were historically unprofitable but can now be aggregated at scale using e-commerce and digital marketing. Examples are the growth of specially targeted cosmetic products like **"The Mom's Co" (India), Mama Earth (India), Patanjali (also in India), or The Honest Company (US).** Or artisanal products like **Talenti ice team** (now acquired by Unilever) in the US.

Patanjali has been a notable success in the India market, from inception in 2006 to reaching revenues of $4 billion in 2020. The company has challenged multinationals like **Unilever, Nestle, Colgate** and others by expanding the reach of packaged consumer goods. Using Ayurveda and "natural" as a key differentiator.

It's a trap, however, to of think that all changes are dramatic. Shampoo will be shampoo, and may not see any dramatic disruption. But even here, the profile of consumption has dramatically changed because of the rise of hyper-personalisation.

The emergence of niches like non-toxic, chemical-free, local, natural "ageing care" – "traditional", etc. – represents an opportunity that can be scaled efficiently using digital market tools. As society gains affluence and the share of food, as a proportion of the household expenditure, drops from (as high as) 70%

in the "BOP" ("Bottom of the Pyramid") down closer to 30%, these niches will get more and more interesting.

People will increasingly use products to uniquely distinguish and identify themselves. Can we take advantage of the underlying changes in consumer behaviour (enabled by digital access) to re-imagine our value propositions, much as the companies listed previously have done?

B) Challenge the underlying assumptions

What are the key assumptions people are making about their markets which can be challenged?

Some interesting **examples** from the **domain of war** where assumptions changed dramatically:

1) Cannons were brought in as significant disruptors by Mughal invaders into the rich Indian subcontinent, where everyone assumed wars were fought with swords, elephants and cavalry, with individual honour as paramount.

2) The use of tanks as rapidly manoeuvre-able mobile artillery rendered the fixed Maginot line obsolete in the Second World War.

3) Similarly, the use of drones in the Azerbaijan Armenia conflict in 2020 may have created a significant discontinuity by challenging the assumption that conventional soldiers are key. Unmanned drones operated from a distance, upended these assumptions fundamentally.

- **Uber** challenged the assumption that one needs to own cars to be a large travel company.

- **AirBnB** and **Ola** challenged the assumption that one needs to manage real estate to be a successful hospitality company.

- Mobile phones challenged the assumption that one needs fixed-landline telephones.

- In **governance** and **sustainability** models, one can engage with and include society to create new models of providing services instead of assuming that governments have to unilaterally create them.

Like the use of solar energy to provide rural lighting and sanitation solutions. Or the use of Aadhar (national identity card) linked data stacks and banking services in India to provide access to services across the population.

This will require quite a few thought experiments in each case to identify such assumptions, and thereafter test models to disrupt these assumptions by running small pilots.

C) Re-imagine products to re-define consumer paradigms

We should not allow ourselves to be limited by assumptions and benefits which exist in the conventional world or within our enterprise.

There are several interesting examples to learn from.

- A conversation with Peter Brabeck, the chairman emeritus of Nestlé S.A, revealed a fascinating insight into the story of **Nespresso**.

Nescafé pure, soluble instant coffee was a unique invention by Nestlé which was very successful all over the world in the years following the Second World War. The product cost the consumer roughly five cents per cup.

In the late 70s, the company invented a unique, **proprietary new technology** that could, at the point of consumption, extract coffee liquor under pressure, using steam and hot water, and create a fabulous cup of coffee with rich aroma and a layer of stable "crema" on top. The product was (logically) launched in the same supermarkets where Nescafé was sold. Consumers were quick to reject a cup of coffee that cost ten times as much as their regular cup of Nescafé. The product was quickly delisted by retailers.

Nespresso then had an existential crisis. How to sell a great cup of coffee when retailers were unwilling to stock your product? This was a huge constraint.

They did a lot of experiments. Eventually, they found success when they rein- vented their business model to go directly to hair salons. Then lawyers' offices and consultants. Anywhere where people had time to spare, appreciated a great cup of coffee, and didn't mind the 50-cent price tag.

The model was a success and grew rapidly. The product then migrated into homes. Nespresso set up their famous boutiques to service consumers directly, all the while innovating on new coffee experiences to offer their clients. And they innovated further by offering accessibly priced machines to enable more households to join this unique coffee system.

The advent of the internet and e-commerce meant they now had a completely new access pathway, using big data to scale this model. The company built a "direct-to-consumer" business model, where they made their buyers feel part of an exclusive club, and grew rapidly, going from success to success. They made their starting constraint a key to their re-imagining the entire product and route to market.

They had effectively created a startup within the company!! One that, at the lat- est reading, had sales of US$6.5 billion in 2021!

- Similarly, **the smart phone**.

The **iPod** was invented by Apple and effectively brought together the MP3 player and the "concept" of Napster to download music (but legally, via "itunes") and added functionality to download single songs rather than an entire album. The iPod ecosystem was a huge success.

Eventually, the iPod, in turn, was cannibalised by the **iPhone**, which subsumed all these functionalities and offered more. Apple was not afraid to re-imagine the prod- uct and value space in a manner which made redundant its own cash cow, the iPod!!

From there, it's a short step to the iCloud for storage, thereby locking in users with personalised and safe, confidential access to their data.

- **Netflix**: A late entrant in the video rentals space where Blockbuster was the leader, Netflix moved early into digital distribution of their content to become a dominant global player in this category.

They have now seen an opportunity to not only create proprietary content tailored to each geographic niche, but have created a "wormhole" into the fast-growing gaming industry, using this loyal customer base.

> Re-imagine what one could do with one's assets. The traditional physical assets, as well as the emerging ones, data. Customer relationships.
>
> Can a business use this "pipeline" where they look at the access to the consumer, to add new products and services?
>
> Opportunity gazing: Keep looking at startups and adjacent markets to identify new trends which might help expand the company's footprint by creating "wormholes" into adjacencies. Like Netflix has done.

Each immersive gaming experience is unique to the player, thus locking them in for longer spans of time. Each time a player returns, they discover something new.

Similarly, Apple has now entered this world with proprietary content and gaming on the metaverse.

How can we learn from these examples and re-imagine our value propositions? Like Nespresso, can we make our constraints the key to our strengths? Or like Netflix and Apple, can we create wormholes into adjacent categories? Keep an eye out for startups doing experiments where they reassemble benefit bundles in new ways: one of these could be the next "smart phone" equivalent disruption!!

D) Imagine fresh consumer paradigms to create a new value space

a. How can we transform social networks and friendship into an economic value proposition and market it as a product? **Facebook, Instagram, Snapchat, Twitter,** and others have created completely new value spaces and ecosystems. Products and spaces which didn't even exist earlier. Or weren't valued economically, though they existed socially.

b. TikTok, as a short-form video sharing platform, has unleashed millions of creative amateur artists to produce their own content and has spread virally with the use of humour.

c. The rise of **gaming** as a major industry as more people access on line games. People are selling "wearables" in the metaverse, priced in cryptocurrencies, taking gaming to a new level, and allowing people to experience virtual reality. People could potentially use avatars in the metaverse to recreate and reimagine their "virtual" lives.

d. Even banks like JP Morgan and consultants like BCG have opened "offices" in the metaverse.

e. **Apple Watch** and **Fitbit** are key future drivers of health care paradigms, even as the wearable device linked to the smart phone becomes the biggest disruptor in future health care. (See Chapter 8 for details.)

f. The invention of **T20 cricket** as a multibillion dollar, fast growing sports industry illustrates the potential of a new paradigm.

    Cricket was a sport designed for a different era, with games being played over a leisurely five days. The demand of a time-efficient model to suit the modern age meant people were shifting away to other sports. Enter a "re-imagining" of the game as a "20 over" format played over a tight three-hour window. This expanded the audience and television franchise and led to the creation of fast-growing T-20 leagues in several countries. The IPL T-20 cricket league in India is now reportedly valued at over US$10 billion!

g. The Swiss company Livinguard AG has used technology to re-imagine and create "non-biocidal" coatings that are self-disinfecting, with anti-bacterial and anti-viral properties, and can be used across a variety of surfaces. When applied to masks, one has reusable and washable masks that are clinically certified to deactivate the Covid virus, among others.

    The technology has a wide variety of applications in hospitals and the hygiene industry and promises to disrupt this space dramatically while making it more ecologically safe by reducing waste and leaching chemicals into water bodies.

h. Any industry can change. Locks were a physical concept for millennia. Security and locks are now going digital and are often biometrics enabled to personalise one's "key".

    About the only advice we can offer here is to benchmark these new developments, of which there are several each week, in some part of the world. And ask if we could use a similar approach to re-imagine our business model.

3. THE ACTION MANTRA

a. Today, more than ever, we need to **lead** with what is happening in the market, by mining the mother lodes of disruption and then (and then only) looking at competition or traditional company strengths. Don't start with the "inside-out" approach based on traditional strengths. The changes underway are far more dramatic than we at first suppose.

b. We are not suggesting that businesses copy blindly. Rather, use what is happening elsewhere to **inspire,** and try to tease out the underlying principle these disruptions are leveraging. Then ask how this principle could be applied to a given industry.

c.   Be open to challenging assumptions that are so basic one doesn't even realise one is making them. This allows space for truly disruptive models.

d.   Disruption is much more likely to happen – and to happen sooner in some sectors than others. The move to services is a classic example. Even for classic consumption products, service and delivery have often transformed experience and thereby the product.

e.   We deliberately don't offer a tool kit. Rather, we have offered a simple framework within which we highlight several success stories. We hope these will inspire the reader to re-invent new and proprietary business models.

Technology is further catalysing changes in consumer lives, as we saw in part II. Next, we'll examine how this is happening and how use of tech enablers and delivery (in itself) can modify the product and market, as services are re-imagined.

NOTE

1   Here is a link: www.nationalgeographic.com/environment/article/how-to-brew-a-greener-beer

Chapter 14

The Re-imagination of Enterprise

Leveraging Technology to Drive Disruption

"The great growling engine of change – technology"
– Alvin Toffler, Futurologist

In our world of epochal change, we find inspiring examples of market disruptions and seizing opportunities, reinforcing the mantra of **"Challenge. Re-imagine. Imagine Anew".**

Powerful, new, emerging technologies are the central force that make this change epoch so disruptive, enabling us to do different things and also do things differently. These technologies give wings to our imagination and the power to bring them to life!

We've just looked at a market-led discovery of opportunities. Here, we're pushing the boundaries of technology to find our possibilities, focusing on technology and delivery: How and where does it make a difference? And, how to extract the technology advantage?

1. THE BUSINESS ADVANTAGE OF TECHNOLOGY

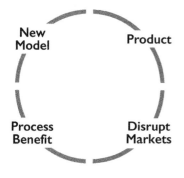

New Model · Product · Disrupt Markets · Process Benefit

The application of technology is changing enterprise in significant ways – in its products, markets, processes, as well as the competitive models it uses to create advantage.

Here is a framework and several examples that can facilitate creating this advantage.

A) Harnessing the power of technology to address chronic problems

New, technology-based and data-driven solutions can be applied to address chronic challenges.

- Low-cost mobile technologies have promoted widespread digital and financial inclusion across the world.

DOI: 10.4324/9781003254737-17

- Covid. Digital connectivity reimagined the workplace to create productive, collaborative, and connected working environments in the face of the most dramatic disruption the world has seen in recent times.

- **Aadhar,** the data stack created by the government of India, is the world's largest biometric identification system. Providing a secure, highly credible, and quick online validation of identity, it has revolutionised the access of over a billion Indians to banking and financial services and social welfare schemes (through direct-benefit transfers). With new uses growing every day, this digital technology has revolutionised the entire canvas of everyday interactions of commerce, governance, and delivery of solutions to individuals across all levels of society.

- These examples highlight how technology can be harnessed to deliver disruptive solutions to challenges and address unsolved problems and emerging opportunities for enterprise and society.

B) Technology by itself can catalyse enhanced and new solutions

Organisations are developing new technologies to **re-imagine** products and services.

- **Wysa** uses AI technologies to re-imagine mental health solutions. Interactive voice technologies, AI-powered diagnostics, and clinically validated therapies help meet mental health challenges of today's world with this accessible solution (without straining resources of specialists).

- Amazon, the world's largest retailer, is founded on the technological creation of virtual marketplaces in the metaverse.

  This can transform a wide range of industries, drawing upon deep insights of markets and shoppers. Examples range from **Etsy** (handmade items, accessories, and more!) to **Medika Bazaar** (a B2B hospital supplies business) to **Naukri.com** (job search) – virtually no domain is left untouched. Emerging technologies like "recommendation engines" and graphic interfaces, often based on improved capabilities in supply chain, logistics, and hybrid business models, are creating new benefit paradigms.

- As we've seen, breakthrough products or services, re-imagined using new technology, create new market opportunities. For example, Netflix, seeking to target the personal entertainment market and avoid the inconvenience in DVD rentals, used connectivity to leapfrog Blockbuster by delivering content directly in-home.

- Even categories that may seem immune to dramatic disruption, like colour cosmetics and beauty care, are being affected. Markets are changing dramatically, driven by online market places that enable mass customisation.

"Direct to consumer" online businesses like **MyGlamm** cater to the rise of hyper-personalisation.

Cure Skin is a startup that uses an artificial intelligence engine, supported by a team of consultants, to diagnose and recommend skin care solutions. Mass-market consumers, using a simple app, can get customised solutions, with dermatological advice that is not otherwise available. High satisfaction and repeat-usage rates result from the use of well-known skin science with the added power of AI and connectivity.

- However, not all changes need be dramatic. We have seen how a relatively small technological shift, low unit-price packs (or sachets in personal care), and telecom (prepaid packs) have driven unprecedented category penetration and market disruption across developing countries.

Harnessing innovation with a consumer focus continues to be the driving force; and now, we have a much stronger and wider technological suite to re-imagine delivery of benefits.

Some of the biggest disruptions are where technology has enabled new realities:

- Many of the most profitable and influential businesses of today have been founded by creatively pushing technology application boundaries. The internet, or social media and messaging apps, are iconic examples of **new products and markets** that previously were unimaginable.

- **New, collaborative benefits are emerging.** Connectivity is enabling powerful platforms (like marketplaces or open-sourced innovation platforms) where multiple stakeholders can come together to collaborate on delivery of benefits to consumers. Or imagining new product and service paradigms.

Innoviti is an emerging fintech enterprise. Its transactions platform enables multiple stakeholders to collaborate. Banks, brands, and merchants can come together to offer a collaborative financing method or a brand promotion, all customised with intelligence, for a specific shopper.

- **New genre of products:** Data itself becomes a product, as discussed in detail in Chapter 9. Knowledge providers are delivering analytics to help reshape industries.

The emergence of affordable **genetic sequencing** has created a **"big data"** play where pharma companies can partner with researchers to create targeted drug regimens for disease clusters. Personalised medicine and nutrition are but an extension of this. The startup Anuva, for example, based across Singapore and Oxford in London, is focusing on developing markets, starting with South Asia, to create a data set of this vast, genetically diverse pool (where none exists yet) in partnership with pharmaceutical companies who screen for illnesses and cures.

- **Opportunities created by emerging technologies:** Foundational new technologies, such as 5G networks, are attracting trillions of dollars in investment worldwide. Transformations of this kind happen with involvement of a wide variety of players that work together. At one end are the core technology developers, the equipment providers, and software and algorithm developers. Infrastructure and the telecom service providers give it an operational reality and deliver the services. At the other end, developers of platforms and applications close the loop to provide consumer benefits. All links within the chain are essential, mutually interdependent, and provide multiple opportunities.

  As **Gopal Vittal, CEO of Airtel India**, advises encouragingly, "Think ecosystems and platforms. Not just products".

  The migration of data storage and processing power to the "cloud" – another example of a large infrastructure transformation – is currently seeing three of the largest companies (Google, Microsoft, and Amazon), as well as a host of other service providers, jostling to capture the opportunity.

C) Using tech to disrupt markets

The prime question in the mind of every market insurgent is "How could I disrupt my market?". In a world of disruptive change, astute incumbents also ask themselves, "How could my business be re-invented for greater success?".

Here are some ways smart use of tech is helping organisations gain disruptive advantage:

- Identify gaps in the handoffs along traditional value chains or where middlemen are cornering value by information arbitrage. Online trading platforms like **Charles Schwab** that allow retail investors to trade and hold financial instruments at a fraction of the cost charged by banks are a good example.

- Look for "niches" which were historically unprofitable but can now be aggregated at scale using e-commerce and digital marketing. Examples are the growth of "non-toxic" cosmetics for pregnant women, like **The Mom's Co (India)**.

- Spot possibilities of disruption in extended value chains, especially in product access and fulfilment. Perhaps the food we eat is not changing fundamentally, but food delivery services like Uber Eats, Zomato, and Swiggy are transforming consumer lifestyles.

In short, we should look for the dominant logic in the market, often formed by years of habit and the absence of alternatives. Then apply the emerging technology pivots and see how the industry value chain could be reimagined.

D) Business process transformation

Technology is opening up a continuum for businesses, from improving functional efficiencies to transformed processes that deliver a competitive advantage. Two fundamental forces are driving a revamping of core business processes:

- Technology applied to internal business processes is giving significant benefits in unit operations, in processes, and in product delivery. We would do well to seek out how we can drive efficiencies and streamline operations using technology.

- Further, ubiquitous connectivity has triggered a fundamental shift. Consumers are now connected continuously. Businesses can engage at virtually every click. These new possibilities are compelling organisations to thoroughly re-imagine business processes and integrate overall operations with higher consumer-centricity.

Here are some examples of business process transformations, starting first with sales/marketing and supply chains:

• The marketing process is changing in fundamental ways

— Marketing becomes more and more about customer acquisition and managing customer lifetime journey and value. As a result, customer persuasion, acquisition, and fulfilment are converging. Not only does supply chain ownership and control of the value chain extend all the way to the consumer, it becomes an integral part of the marketing process by helping create customer delight.

— The emergence of connected commerce/smart commerce, both omni-channel and online, means that marketers have to be able to influence consumers at the **moment of purchase**, whenever that might be.

   Direct access to the consumer and "moments of truth" are driving **hyper-personalisation** while consumers shop on digital marketplaces from the convenience of home.

   "Big data" is an emerging foundation for marketing that uses intelligence. Netflix suggests movies to us based on our viewing habits, or Amazon suggests books. This is smart use of data to increase consumption through the power of suggestion. Consumption patterns are shifting as a result.

— Selling, even in the B2B context, is taking on a new avatar and going digital. Companies like Indogene are helping pharma majors improve sales effectiveness and economies with digital "medical representatives". Even events like the Farnborough International Air Show are connecting digitally.

— Changes in media consumption and influence patterns (articulated in Chapter 8) demand that marketers become adept at orchestrating "many to many" conversations that consumers have about one's brand, and in real time.

— With increasing saturation of digital media (and the fact that we are over-loaded with marketing messages throughout the day), experiential marketing starts to gain traction. Whether it is Emirates sponsoring demonstration events inside football stadiums or the KitKat "chocolatory" boutique, one way to engage with consumers is to create a unique and unexpected "Aha" experience in the "real" world.

A related and emerging media vector is the "consumer hotline". Formerly a "problem resolution metric", it is now morphing to a brand advocacy vehicle, taking a consumer with a complaint and delivering an "Aha" response that converts the complainant into a brand advocate. While Zappos is often held up as a best practice in this area, even legacy companies like Gerber have built core competence in this area.

Even as we feel that everything has changed, the fundamentals of marketing and sales remain the same. Good propositions, delivering value and connecting the consumer "moments of truth", drive the marketing and sales process like always. The change: new and emerging media vectors that demand a re-think of how we engage with consumers.

• Supply chain, manufacturing, and service delivery: process improvements in efficiency, quality, and more

Supply chains efficiencies are drawing upon connectivity and the addition of intelligence and are being transformed in the process.

In terms of the approach to quality, new technologies are helping. In monitoring the quality of baked cookies or biscuits, for instance, their colour (the golden, baked colour) can be monitored with advances in imaging technologies. With online AI-based systems, quality can now be ensured in every unit (versus sampling-based assurance systems used earlier).

This is true for products and services alike.

IoT (internet of things) applications hold great promise in virtually every supply chain process, within and outside factories. IoT can monitor and improve grain storage in silos too!

• Re-structuring supply chains

The concept of "last-mile assembly" (mentioned earlier in the context of 3D printing) may be a way forward for several products. The pioneers in this, from the supply chain side, were the paint industry, who often blended colours at the point of sale. Or consider newspapers, where digital tech has been used for long to typeset and transfer pages electronically to local editions for physical printing.

Customisation close to the point of sale can amplify taste and flavour. After all, fresh food does taste better!! We see examples in coffee machines like Nespresso or Kuerig. We fully expect other products like pizza or yoghurt or sauces to be customised at close to the delivery and consumption point.

This is being carried forward further to industries with high distribution costs, such as the furniture business (witness IKEA).

• *Every process can change*

Digital technologies are transforming industry-specific processes to **unlock new benefits**.

The use of blockchain to improve traceability of the finished product is a good example. Today, we can use blockchain to trace a can of milk powder back to the farm (and even the specific cow) from which it was originally sourced.

A similar approach can be used for battery replacement cycles in the emerging EV space.

Crowd sourcing of innovation is an intriguing new idea. In finance, forensic accounting based on big data can discover irregularities or corruption. The growth of fintech has transformed commercial and transactional processes.

E) New business models: transformed businesses and a new organisational DNA

Disruptive changes in consumer and societal behaviours, driven by technology, are triggering new business models. These are not merely different ways of doing business, but they are often recreating the product offering and, in many cases, the very DNA of the business. Some of the primary themes of change are:

• *Re-imagining products as service*

An emerging opportunity is to "re-imagine products as a service". After all, one is really interested in the service provided by the refrigerator (or TV or air conditioner) and similar durables, rather than the product per se. Even for classical consumption products, service and delivery can transform customer experience and thereby the product experience.

"Product as a service" (examples in succeeding paragraphs) and "productisation of services" are new, invented terms to describe this emerging opportunity (the "service" of investing in mutual funds are marketed as a product, for example). Companies as diverse as Rolls Royce, Philips, and H&M are adopting this concept to re-imagine business models.

The World Economic Forum also discusses the "product as service" business model in response to the challenge of sustainability, where companies are expected to retain control and take responsibility for the "end of life" impact of their products (maybe years after they have sold it).

For several years now, Rolls Royce has followed a model where they do not sell aircraft engines; they prefer selling "running hours", whereby the company takes responsibility of repairs, replacement, and maintenance.

Apparently, Michelin has already started experimenting with such a service for large fleets of cars or trucks. If that is possible for tyres, then where else could this model lead? BMW have announced plans for a similar model for cars, where a factory is set up to "recycle" cars by design.

Could this model be expanded to consumer durables? After all, none of us wish to indefinitely own refrigerators or air conditioners or cars. We are, however, very interested in the use of these assets. Could consumer durable manufacturers "sell usage" of the asset and then take it back at the end of its usable life? Mobile phones, anyone?

• *Asset fungibility drives new business models*

Individual assets are being harnessed, connecting together local enterprise into big networks orchestrated by a central core. Oyo (hotels rooms), Uber, and Airbnb have been prime examples of this move. In a similar manner, Uberisation of tractors and farm equipment is an interesting idea being tried out by startups in rural India. These new, connected businesses often deliver not only better efficiencies (e.g., optimised fleet utilisation across the network) but also superior benefits (e.g., convenient ride hailing).

• *Business models leverage new-age connectivity*

The growth of connectivity is re-shaping industry models. "Direct to consumer" models and better-integrated "business to business to consumer" models (B2B2C) are transforming industries by disrupting value delivery, along with significant cost and customer access benefits.

Medical imaging companies feed specialised information to practitioners and hospitals. Mpharma in Africa is a great example of a company that creates a data "triangulation" between the health care provider, the patient, and the pharmaceutical distribution chain to ensure genuine drug availability, compliance with drug regimens, and fair prices for genuine (non-fake) drugs.

Innovative, new models are emerging. Retail trade is increasingly finding advantage in exploring hybrid models combining online selling with on-ground services. Such developments often draw upon "phygital" strengths – digital technologies along with big advancements in physical capabilities, as seen today in courier-based logistics systems. Logistics companies like Delhivery form a vital, supportive link in such models.

Technology is creating a wide spectrum of opportunities for improved delivery and competitive advantage, harnessing innovative process improvements, the adoption of distinct business models, and moving towards a total re-imagination of the business.

2. HOW COULD COMPANIES EXTRACT THE TECHNOLOGICAL ADVANTAGE

A) Creating the disruptive edge with technology

Our starting premise is that **disruption has a consumer foundation**. As Tim O'Reilly says, "What new technology does is create new opportunities to do a job that customers want done"[1].

Technologies, though critical in themselves, get their power in a highly appealing benefit pivot or a game-changing consumer difference they enable.

How do we therefore bring together the prowess of technology with consumer fundamentals to build our disruptive edge? Here is one possible process to re-imagine opportunities (see the following box for a quick summary).

> **CREATING DISRUPTIVE ADVANTAGE**
>
> A) Identify a **pool of consumer pivots** with disruptive potential- big needs, pain points or expectations. A particular focus on our world of change.
>
> B) Understand **technologies AND their potential** to create new benefit pivots.
>
> C) Apply one to the other with the mantra of disruption (**Challenge, Re-imagine, Imagine Anew**). Create new and disruptive solutions.

- **Identify the consumer pivots with disruptive potential** – the big needs (salient or latent), pain points, or even emerging expectations.

  We emphasise a particular focus on the new and the transforming:[2] new consumer groups or demographic profiles of societal change or even new products paradigms (like assisted living) that are resonating with today's world. Big needs have remained unaddressed so long that they have recessed in consumer articulation. Bringing to surface a latent delight that has not even been imagined is another option.

- **Understand emerging technologies**, their powerful new possibilities, and the benefit pivots they could unleash.

  Draw upon the essential human impact of the "disruptive" technologies visible across multiple domains (see how smart phones and connectivity help us to do every day behaviours anywhere, anytime).

  Equally, consider the changing ground rules and possibilities specific to your category (an example is the transformation being triggered with "in-home" learning in education.).

- **Apply this understanding** of technology benefits and potential pivots (in business models or product applications) to consumer disruption nodes to create new business opportunities. Take each emerging technology and see what difference it could make, applied in your domain of interest, your industry or value space, the need area for your consumer or society, or even your business processes where you wish to imagine a new reality.

The vital difference in this application is **our mantra of disruption**. Challenging the current realities and shaping them creatively to unleash a disruptive edge. In many cases, several emerging technologies could come together to deliver powerful new benefits. For example, the growing adoption of virtual assistants (with an almost humanoid appeal) draws upon voice recognition advances, AI-based interaction engines, IoT devices, and the "cloud".

B) Harnessing the dynamic world of technology

How could we focus our efforts and take advantage of emerging tech advances? (The following box has an abbreviated summary.)

TECHNOLOGY- CORE TO STRATEGY AND OPERATIONS

Recognise critical impact for every business

- Shapes consumers, products markets, and our opportunities

- Efficiencies, processes, and models.

Systematically scan and understand

- Disruptive advances

- Cross applications abound. Look across a band of tech.

- Understand the tech. And the benefit pivot: what "is the customer difference".

Use. With focussed strategy and execution

- Use. Ask where tech makes a consumer or business difference.

- Learn from disruptors and use cases, in your industry but also across others.

- There is a lot lying on the table. Apply it. Discover the new.

- Create the conviction, capability and commercial advantage.

- **Recognise the critical technological difference**

Identify how tech is creating new products and markets, and further, how it's shaping consumer lives and expectations. Recognise the difference it is making in business models, efficiencies, and competitive deliveries.

The tumult of technology is creating **the** difference for business survival and success.

- **Scan and understand technological** advances systematically and across a broad spectrum.

New generations of technology are emerging and impacting large swathes of industries. Consider how the move from 2G to 4G to 5G in mobile connectivity has widened the metaverse and bought in breakthrough new applications.

New product platforms are becoming pivots of further change. Fintech services are not only re-imagining financial institutions – the entire world of commerce is changing. Streetside hawkers now accept payments using Google Pay!!

Technologies have a strong ripple effect, sometimes in unexpected areas. 3D printing, at first, seemed to be just a process development with an industrial or functional appeal. But it has opened a new world of customised products available instantly. A technology which was never available earlier (in the era of assembly-line manufacture) now enables last-mile assembly, or customisation, as discussed earlier.

Or consider electricity-powered aircrafts. Demonstration flights are already underway. Its impact goes far beyond an alternate propulsion system to radically changing the design of aircrafts – and airports!

So, we should continuously scan the rapidly changing world of technology, understand it, and draw out consumer and business implications.

- **Apply tech with a focused strategy and execution**

A focused strategy is vital, given the wide set of technology choices and its potential impact on a re-imagined business. Technological competencies need time to develop. Capability and conviction, along with a longer-term plan of using it for advantage, is needed to deliver commercial success.

C) Technology – a philosophy and a belief

Many variables drive the success of any enterprise. In this chapter, we have chosen to focus on technology.

It is our conviction that, in these times of disruptive change, technology is **THE** difference that will drive future success and in a variety of ways: how we deliver and how we capture market opportunities for our products, processes, and business models; for efficiencies; for consumer delight; and more!

Technology is a fast-evolving space with myriad possibilities. We are struck by several inspiring examples that engage with it far beyond its technical complexity to harness it with **imagination, insight, and a strong consumer focus**. We hope these examples inspire you to explore more and find the technology leverage that works for your business.

Every market can change. Every business and process can change. A positive bias for change helps. If you appear untouched so far, look harder; there is an opportunity waiting to be discovered.

Technology is emerging to be central to enterprise. Successful organisations of today have a technological core at their heart: a strategy, mindset, and processes to "scan it" and "build it". They use it imaginatively and improve it continuously to seize this epochal opportunity.

3. ENTERPRISE AND THE CHALLENGE OF CHANGE

• A re-imagination of the core of the business

In this section, we have seen how big disruptions are driving a change in enterprise, its products, markets, and how it leverages technology to do its business.

It is our contention that it is not just individual elements of our business that are changing. The fundamental essence of every business itself is getting transformed.

The ultimate impact of disruptive change for enterprise is felt at its strategic core. Its fundamental choices of WHO do we add value to, WHAT is it that we offer, and HOW do we deliver on it with maximum consumer impact.

- We see new consumer cohorts and a transformation of society accelerated by tech-driven behaviours. Consumer lives are getting redefined, as are product expectations. Value spaces are morphing and new markets emerging to grow rapidly. A redefined customer focus has to drive the re-imagination of every company's products and markets.

- We see big shifts in "what" even the largest companies focus on: Microsoft has pivoted its business to leverage "cloud" based opportunities.

  Others are imaginatively pivoting to new markets, finding "wormholes" that give them a strategic advantage into new markets. An example is Netflix or Apple or Microsoft finding its way into gaming.

  Often, new companies are growing like bean stalks, sharp focussing on their (new) markets of choice. Genies, a very recent unicorn, prides itself as culture's leading avatar technology company, empowering humans to create their own avatar ecosystems. Akash Nigam, its CEO, says, "With every advancement of the internet, an expansive new region of entrepreneurial skill sets is born. In Web3, Gen Z avatar ecosystem builders are going to be the leaders of innovation . . . we strive to empower their wildest imaginations, ideas, and experiences as avatar creations".

- Companies are disrupting markets with a new set of assets (including data), technologies, business models, and competencies. Data is the new asset, and intelligence (especially AI), the new capability. A capability not just to monetise data, but to utilise it to deliver better value to our core customers.

  Today, customer relationships are the most valued asset of businesses that focus on customer lifetime value maximisation. A successful motto is to "own the pipeline to the consumer, be fanatical about building loyalty and use this as a platform for growth".

  In the process, create new products and uncover new markets. Says Gopal Vittal, CEO of Airtel, "Getting more consumers, increasing their stickiness by delivering better to them, and getting to meet more of their needs, drives our strategic actions".

Businesses are quickly adopting foundational new capabilities by developing strategic technologies and digital marketing/sales skills to drive success.

• The challenge of leadership

Many companies merely wonder or speculate what change is coming their way. However, successful leadership understands the disruptions, identifies its choices, and drives to reinvent its deliveries, models, and capabilities for success.

We wish to reiterate the enormity of the changes and the need to lead with "what is happening in the market". To repeat: Mine the mother lodes of disruption, and then (and then only), look at competition or traditional company strengths. Don't start with the "inside-out" approach based on traditional strengths. And, power your choices with the mantra of "Challenge, Re-imagine, and Imagine Anew". The changes underway are far more dramatic than we at first suppose.

• *Leadership has to contend with three*
big issues, which we explore more in the next chapter

1. Conviction and drive. The Company has to make daring choices, riding a maelstrom of change, and execute some fundamental shifts. From the comfort of today, a leap for tomorrow.

2. There is scale, criticality, and complexity in the change within, and all to be carried out in a short time. The transformation of the organisation: What is the change we seek, and how to make it happen?

3. To manage the everyday business and to simultaneously transform itself for the opportunity are two big and very different objectives. How does business resolve the issues and dilemmas between these two existential tugs?

As authors, we believe this last mile of actually seizing the change and making it happen is what makes the difference. In our next, and capstone, chapter, we will look at the significance of leadership and organisation building, and examine the big issues involved.

NOTES

1   We could add to this jobs that the consumer has never thought of getting done but would be delighted to be surprised with. New technologies can indeed create highly valued benefits, some of which may not have ever been imagined or stated!

2   A vital input is a deep understanding of change and its consumer manifestations. As a starting point, draw upon different aspects of the big societal and technological shifts, as highlighted in the first two parts of the book.

    Also, you could use the big themes that define the new world of the consumer: their world view, emerging product paradigms, and how change is impacting the various domains of their life (Chapter 12).

Chapter 15

Re-imagine Organising
Lead to Seize the Win

"The greatest danger in times of turbulence is not the turbulence itself, it's to act with yesterday's logic."

– Peter Drucker

We live in a world of ever-accelerating "disruption", coming at us from a surprising diversity of directions. Re-imagination and transformation of enterprises' products, markets, and technologies is the driving engine for success.

And, leadership and organising will be **the** vital difference to deliver onto the challenges of re-imagination of enterprise. The key question is **"How?"**. How do we reorganise to win while the tsunami of the "What" (the disruptions) bears down on us. **Re-imagine organisations**. Business processes. Business models. And more.

Success requires us to master the inherent tensions and re-imagine how we organise to seize the opportunity, even while we continue to operate our businesses efficiently.

We recognise that nobody is immune to this. Disruption will impact the mainstream of business and not appear only on the fringes. The change is rapid, complex, and risky. We need to act now with clarity, nimbleness, and conviction to seize the moment.

The entire canvas of enterprise will change, as startups gain greater salience (we discuss startups in a separate appendix to this chapter). "Beanstalks" (see box in the Appendix) will shoot up, rapidly gaining size, and incumbents will learn to dance nimbly like startups.

We attempt to cover a lot of ground; this is a condensed bible (a "go to" chapter) for people desiring to seize this epochal opportunity. Rather than go into great depth analysing any one approach, we share a palette of questions and choices that one may wish to adapt, for the stage the organisation is in.

In doing so, we bring to bear perspectives and insights drawn from successful global multinationals, experiences with start-ups and venture capitalists, and also concepts from academic thinkers and literature.

DOI: 10.4324/9781003254737-18

MANAGING THE INHERENT TENSIONS TO "SEIZE THE WIN"

Hidden within this question of "How can companies organise and 'seize a Win'" are three underlying tensions of leadership that have to be managed and balanced. We will look at each in turn.

- **The leadership "stance" and inherent strategic tensions**

- **The leadership tensions in organising for insurgency**

- **Leading through the "how" of change**

We look at how business models can be recreated and how managers can be trained to navigate these tensions.

I. THE LEADERSHIP "STANCE" AND INHERENT STRATEGIC TENSIONS

Disruption will affect all aspects of life and business, as we have seen in the first two parts of this book. Ignoring it is not an option. Startups and insurgents will gain greater salience. And, as they grow and attract intellectual capital (which is the fuel of this epoch of creative disruption), they will influence large incumbents to change the way they operate. Or risk becoming dinosaurs, or relics of their past.

The changes coming will affect mainstream business and not occur only on the fringes. What is important is to learn, unlearn, and re-learn constantly. Experiment. Fail fast. Survive. And scale fast. Fortune will favour the prepared.

As we recognise the urgency created by this "epochal tsunami of disruption", the key questions for any business faced with disruption are highlighted in the following box.

BUSINESS FACED WITH DISRUPTION NORMALLY ASK SEVERAL QUESTIONS?
- How can we **prepare better** for this Epoch of Disruption?
- Should we be the disruptor and first mover who creates a market?
- Or is the winner the fast follower who scales faster? After all Google wasn't the first search engine. It was simply the best!!
- Are the rules for success in an epoch of disruption different for startups versus established companies?
- How can we reimagine and respond to this tsunami of disruption…or transform a running business?
- What about "beanstalks" (unidimensional, fast growing startups)?
- How about incumbents under attack from disruptors. Are they all destined to go the way of Kodak?
All very valid questions

As these questions highlight, there are several tensions at a strategic level:

A) The tension in the source of the next big disruption

Is it likely from your competitors . . . or will it be from outside your industry?

Any of the disruptive changes discussed in parts I and II of this book could dramatically alter the shape of the market one serves.

Electricity was a key enabler of disruptive technologies and business models in 1900. So much so that many companies then had **"Vice Presidents of Electricity"**.

Today, we find that concept laughable. But in a very similar vein, today we have companies with **"Vice Presidents of Technology"** (or CTO). And once having set up these functions, they are then incentivised on cost control, efficiency, etc. Familiar things that we can control.

From the board level down, we need people who understand that tech (and possibly "sustainability") are the new "electricity", and will affect ALL aspects of the company business models and strategy.

On board people who have exposure to the startup universe, to disruption, to new technologies, and get them to spark introspection and re-invention within.

- The size of the segment, their expectations, as they evolve, age, or urbanise.

- Or as they get familiar with the use of AR and VR technologies.

- Or even new opportunities that may be created by **technological** evolution.

Each will have ripple effects that cascade across several industries (often unrelated).

Companies that take note, move, and experiment fast will create disruptive and winning business models.

The disruption that drives your model into obsolescence may not come from your industry but from a completely different field, which simply redefines current customer expectations.

An area the authors believe is likely to be a significant source of disruptions is the ESG response. Specifically, as businesses evolve to "product as service" models (see Chapter 14 on re-imagining delivery) where they take responsibility for the entire value chain and lock in customers for an extended period of time and usage (making them less receptive to more external disruption), ESG might well be the next "digital".

So, an important requirement for the future CEO (or CTO, or indeed, board members) is to have one eye constantly on the horizon to see what is going on out there.

If they see the disruption coming far off, then they have time to prepare a variety of responses.

B) The tension between responding to the disruption as a threat . . . or as an opportunity

Should one respond to the disruption (irrespective of whether you were the originator, like Kodak) as if it were a threat?

> **Kodak** is a famous case study. As the Eastman Kodak company, they were a Chemicals powerhouse at the turn of the last century. They invented the box camera in 1888, and then dominated the photography market through the next 100 years. Through innovations like colour photography, movie photography and so on.
>
> In 1975, they invented digital photography and saw this as the next big disruptor. For the next 20 years they focused on this new opportunity only to find their business model was not commercially viable. They were trying to get people to capture digital images, and then print these on Kodak Paper.
>
> **People just didn't. Print.**
>
> Roughly 20 years later, Kodak closed down this division and went back to focus on its core, paper based photography.
>
> In 2012 the company **filed for bankruptcy** and has seen its treasure trove of patents being acquired since then.

This would mean finding a way to protect current business cash flows and customers, cutting costs, and focussing to stay viable and competitive.

Or should one respond to it as if it were an opportunity? Invest in the disruption and put all one's resources to chasing it.

The case of Kodak (see box), as contrasted to the response of Fujifilm (now still a successful global multinational), provides some direction.

As opposed to Kodak, who first chased the opportunity and then pivoted years later to focus on their core paper business (the "threat" based response), Fujifilm, on the other hand, did both.

They focussed on their core businesses, cut costs, stayed competitive in protecting their core, while simultaneously seeking opportunities in leveraging the new digital photo tech. Today, they are a successful global multinational who are leaders in paper-based photo printing as well as digital medical imaging and thin film technology applications.

The Chinese word "*weiji*" (see symbol), which means "crisis", has two characters. The first represents "danger"; the second, "opportunity". The lesson is that a crisis presents both. It is up to us to choose one response or the other. Or both.

The learning for business is that, faced with any crisis or disruption, look at **both** responses. The "threat" response is first to protect core customers, cash flow, and businesses in the short term. And the "opportunity" response is to find ways to leverage the disruption to create competitive advantage, even if it disrupts existing businesses the company may consider to be "core".

A good example, is the company Apple. Of course, in the case of Apple and the iPod, the medium-term success of the smart phone opportunity meant that "the then core" business of the iPod was rendered obsolete. And this is a real possibility. Chasing the opportunity might, in time, render one's current business obsolete.

> A classic tension for entrepreneurs is that between **"value creation" and "value capture"**.
>
> Each business starts with passion and a phase of intense experimentation to arrive at the best "value creation" model that best solves the problem one is focusing on.
>
> The business then moves to the "value capture" phase where it tries to scale rapidly. In the process, discouraging re-invention of the historic 'value creation' model.
>
> This tension then permeates the business and entrepreneurs' thinking going forward. Should one focus on value capture to drive financial returns? Or should one re-invent the value creation model?
>
> Or know what is the right time to be ruthless and unemotionally "pull the plug" in order to re-focus resources on parts of the portfolio more likely to respond.
>
> Is it possible to do both at the same time? Or is it necessarily sequential? Please see the references at the end of this chapter for a brief discussion on the "S curve".

Until then, however, do what it takes to stay competitive in the current business. While exploring where the opportunity might lead.

C) Should one BE the disruptor or is it better to be a fast follower?

We have looked at various sources of disruption in parts I and II of this book. It is very tempting to identify the opportunities that emerge (catering to the rapidly rising population of "seniors", for example – or to "refocus efforts on large urban agglomerations using e-commerce").

This is important and potentially a very good strategy, if the opportunity is clearly identifiable. If so, do rapid pilots to test what works, and then scale rapidly.

If a startup, do this piloting below the radar, out of sight of large competitors.

But often, the process of identifying how best to target a new opportunity can consume a lot of resources. And can also fail to identify a clear path to successful commercialisation.

An alternative is to keep a close watch on markets and then follow a successful idea with a better product (service), better customer delivery, and invest resources in rapid scaling.

This approach is better-suited to large companies who have large resources but lack the culture to do rapid experimentation and deal well with failure.

In general, as Prof Costas Markides of London Business School observes, companies can respond in one of five ways. (These are not mutually exclusive; they can often be sequential.)

— Ignore the disruption (can work if the disruptor does not have scale or is hyper local).

— Raise one's quality on the core offering and hope this addresses the disruption (this might work if quality of delivery is the reason why people are switching).

— Borrow the disruptive idea and scale faster, especially in new markets/geographies. For instance, when Nestlé takes the '3 in 1' coffee (powder) mix

---

Shortly before he died, **Steve Jobs** was asked for his views on strategy. He kept quiet for a few minutes, thinking, and then said, "I'm waiting". Encapsulated within that short reply is a great truth.

Apple is probably the most valuable company of our time. And it is held out as an example of "the great disruptor".

But they were not often the first mover. The concept of the computer "mouse" was borrowed from Xerox. The iPod was the MP3 player re-purposed with a great consumer interface, design and a legal on-line library.

The smart phone was invented by others, but Apple saw and unleashed its potential. In the process they had the courage to disrupt their own iPod!

So it's not always the disruptor who wins. The fast followers who scale it better, and with courage, often come out on top.

---

concept from Asia and re-purposes it to be a premium "cappuccino" offering in Europe and other markets. Apple often did this (see box).

— Disrupt the disruptor. Nespresso is a great example of Nestle disrupting the "roast and ground" coffee offerings with proprietary, technology-driven quality, as well as great customer service (delivery).

— Buy the disruptor or partner with the disruptor. Nestle partnering with Starbucks is a good example.

Irrespective of the strategic choice made, a key capability is to learn how to dance with disruption.

2. THE LEADERSHIP TENSIONS IN ORGANISING FOR INSURGENCY

Leadership has two fundamental tasks in today's age of accelerated disruption.

• Managing the current business, cash flows, and customers, and staying viable.

• Preparing the organisation for change. Anticipating change. Leading change.

We have chosen in this chapter to focus on the "tension" between these two and "how to manage this tension" (rather than look at only the first task in great detail).

A) The tension between "run" (to manage the core) and "transform" (to disrupt)

The key question for an incumbent is "how can one organise, to manage the core business while at the same time, respond to the disruption, without taking the eye off either ball?".

Today, every business faces an inherent tension within its operations. The historical need is to "run" the operations efficiently. Especially if one is in the scale-up stage. Incentives, organisation structures, and career paths are designed to reward good performance at this "task" of running organisations efficiently. However, disruption in the environment requires a "transform" mindset.

As an article in the Harvard Business Review in November 2021 suggests, the key might lie in the "project economy" (https://hbr.org/2021/11/the-project-economy-has-arrived).

Because the way forward to respond with agility to ongoing disruptive effects of technology (part II of this book) is necessarily "cross-value-chain", transformational efforts need to be structured around project teams that comprise multiple functions, have a specific task or set of KPI, and are disbanded once the project is complete. Often, these teams might be ad hoc and created to deal with imminent crises.

However traditional career paths and incentive structures do not accord projects the same priority as "running" operations. This mindset needs to evolve, and urgently.

Firstly, business that successfully negotiates ongoing disruptive trends will need to be good at BOTH. "Running" its operations efficiently AND "transforming" its operations and processes through "project teams". Recognising and managing this inherent tension constructively is a key task of leadership.

(It is equally important to shape a culture and nurture leaders who are able to perform their core function while being mindful of the other. Run the business efficiently, for example, while being mindful of projects driving change which might "re-imagine" the business. We will discuss both these tasks at length in the next section of this chapter.)

Secondly, even while "running" operations, companies need to consciously build in a mindset of utilising disruption to advantage:

- Capabilities. (Using technology creatively across routine activities to enhance performance. For example, using blockchain in supply chain to improve quality of forecasting and traceability. Please see the following.)

- Learning agility. How quickly can one learn by looking outside at competitors to identify successful new adaptations and then bring them within? This requires a culture of learning. (See the next section for culture.)

- "Direct to Consumer" (DTC) relationships and data-based marketing and sales models where one captures a larger part of the value chain. The future belongs to companies who can build and nurture healthy lifetime customer relationships. Learning how to capture and (ethically) use data is a key part of this.

- Reverse logistics and recycling models built into the value chain to ensure good "sustainability" practices will start to become a key differentiator.

B) "Organising to win" in disruptive times by designing company capabilities

To succeed at each stage of evolution requires one to understand and build relevant capabilities. We will explore this along four sub-dimensions.

• How is organising changing today

Startups like Google and others in Silicon Valley try their best to retain an "early stage/startup" mindset and culture, even as they scale up to become beanstalks or do M&A deals to expand their breadth of services and offerings. Most have consciously recreated campus environments to foster informality and convenience.

Google famously (before the wave of tech layoffs in early 2023) used to allow employees 20% time to work on their own ideas (ideas not sponsored by the corporate), in order to encourage dreaming and creativity. The idea is to consciously cultivate the "early stage" mindset, even as you scale.

So, a part of the company is always re-inventing.

• The composition and criteria for selection of employees is changing

In addition to emerging requirements to work across cultures and demographics, there is an emerging understanding of the importance of diversity in teams, for social causes as well as business performance reasons.

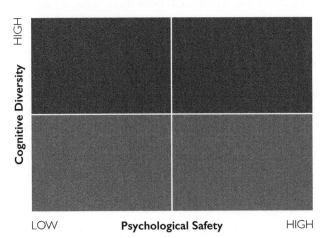

Teams tend to perform better when they have "cognitive diversity" and a leadership that creates "psychological safety" wherein this diversity can be harnessed and leveraged (ref.: HBR article by Reynolds and Lewis).

At the same time, there is growing awareness of laws and regulations to prevent sexual harassment in the workplace. This is an important part of the effort to create the psychological safety within companies that allows them to better harness diversity.

In this YouTube video on how to hire, Eric Schmidt of Google shares his thinking that it is key to hire "talent", even if they are not skilled in your business. Even Mavericks. When they bring great passion and expertise, they will create value by thinking and creating out of the box.

• Innovation in organisation structures

The historical context saw an innovation in organisation, where hundreds of people came together in large offices. Physical proximity allowed rapid communication and alignment. This is now changing. "Work from home", the emerging "gig" economy, and outsourcing are all challenging the previously held organisation design paradigms.

Today, one requires collaboration across boundaries, even for innovation, which is often open sourced. Or the ability to subsume startups and acquired companies.

A key challenge is to try to preserve the spirit of missionary zeal. How to change the world. How to manage chaos in a controlled way. This is one reason many startups get acquired: in order to acquire creators and new talent.

As an organisation, one should consciously choose organisation structures that enable agility and flexibility to manage the strategic tensions described previously. This will mean:

i)   Managing the overall business as a portfolio manager. Different parts of it might need different tools and approaches to succeed. This includes the ability to let go of parts of the portfolio that do not fit the strategy or competencies going forward.

ii) Choosing leaders to fit the stage of business for each part of the portfolio.

iii) Choosing organisation structures flexibly, between the "run" mode and project teams to "transform"; and creating incentives, KPI, and career paths that recognise this dual approach.

iv) Consciously develop a capability to learn from other organisations. Whether they be competitors or those acquired through M&A. Make lifelong learning a part of your people-development processes.

v)   Put in place a capability to do small experiments, pilots, where one can test, fail, learn, and iterate to success. Without penalties.

• Innovations in communication (or even co-creation) with customers

The previous generation of mass media saw "one to many" communications on prime-time programs dominate. This was a key competency for companies to acquire and excel in. Today, communication has morphed. From "one to many", moving to "one to one" (CRM, call centres), it has moved to "many to many", as discussed earlier.

A key competency to acquire, therefore, is, "How to orchestrate consumers in a 'many to many' communication universe". As we have discussed earlier, today's consumer is driven by "ratings and reviews".

Consciously build in this thinking into the way one connects with customers and consumers. This approach may vary between different parts of the portfolio, depending on what "stage" they are in.

C) Shaping the cultural energy of your company

Specific lessons for incumbents. Companies who are historically good at scaling face a key challenge. How to re-acquire the insurgent mindset? How to play multiple games simultaneously?

One of the pitfalls established companies fall into is to try and support "transformational", new businesses within the existing structure. Given that anything truly transformational may well destroy the old business model, the organisation (culture, incentives, career paths) is quick to develop "antibodies" that serve to throttle the new idea.

A good method to insulate the new concept is to separate it into a "skunk works" disguised as a "pilot", with a separate office, people, culture, budget, KPI, incentive plan, and leadership.

Apple has demonstrated an ability to do this and create new innovations (as mentioned earlier, the iPhone destroyed the iPod).

It is important, in that case, to know "how to lead across multiple skunk works" without alienating existing core businesses that may be disrupted.

One way companies try to re-acquire insurgent and "early-stage culture"/

NAYAMED AND MEDTRONIC

In 2012, Medtronic decided to set up Nayamed as a new and creative way to offer hospitals access to quality economy range of pacemakers and defibrillators.

The vision was grand. This new unit would extend reach and tap into a completely new market opportunity.

The reality was however very different, as sales people and others in the parent company saw this insurgent as a threat, and took steps that challenged the success of this new business model.

Ref: Case study discussed by Prof Costas Markides at LBS.

business models is by acquiring new companies or startups. It is a path that has mixed results because, according to studies, the majority of acquisitions fail to create value for the acquirer.

A key competency the company needs will be the ability to integrate the new startups or acquired companies and scale them without compromising what made them successful in the first place. Such as their culture, their sense of purpose, and missionary zeal.

Failure to account for this and a haste to "integrate" brings with it obvious dangers (like L'Oréal and Anita Roddick's Body Shop, where the integration destroyed value).

Or they may choose to keep the acquired startups at arm's length (like Unilever with Dollar Shave Club), in order to preserve their culture, independence, and growth models. While using their big company competencies and scale to support them in the back office.

Industry leaders like Nestle have demonstrated that it is possible to manage a portfolio of businesses across several geographies and life-stages. And create structures that allow each to be played according to its rules and life-stage.

3. LEADING THROUGH THE "HOW" OF CHANGE

A) How does one create a culture that encourages "defending the core" with a culture that encourages "re-imagining for the new opportunity created by disruption"?

For incumbents faced with disruption, the challenge is: How does one create a culture that encourages "defending the core" with a culture that encourages "re-imagining for the new opportunity created by disruption"? How can you build "learning agility" into your organisation?

- There has to be an understanding that different parts of the business may be in different stages, and a key role of the executive board is to be the "portfolio manager", who staff and play each business according to the success requirements for the stage that part of the portfolio is in.

- It is equally important to understand that company culture evolves and changes at each stage of life. There is therefore a need for periodic and conscious evaluation and reinvention of company or sub-unit culture to suit each stage of the business.

- Culture in most companies is initially defined by the founders and promoters. Often, these are maverick inventors. And shared through the company as a "creation mythology" to transfer culture, purpose, and values across generations of managers.

- A famous speech by the late Professor Sumantra Ghoshal, delivered at the World Economic Forum in Davos, is available on YouTube as an eight-minute extract, called "The smell of the place". What he suggests is that four factors come together to create the culture (he calls it "the smell of the place").

    — "Strategy", which can be defined as a box of constraints, or alternatively, in "aspirational stretch" terms.

— "Processes", which can be either compliance or discipline oriented.

— "Team dynamics", which can be either contractual or trust based.

— And "leadership behaviours", which can be either control oriented or support oriented.

It is possible to measure one's culture and then consciously work on these four levers to tailor the company culture. Indeed, the authors have helped companies across business sectors and geographies to do so.

As an insurgent, one requires a culture that supports and encourages mavericks and innovators. In the "scale-up" phase, one requires marketing and sales specialists who can drive growth while controlling innovation. "Maturity" often requires administrators and cost cutters, while the final stage requires negotiators and deal makers who can sell or restructure the portfolio. At every stage, the culture has to evolve.

This becomes even more important in a fast-changing environment, as strategies evolve dynamically. What is important is to be very aware of culture, purpose, and competencies at every stage of growth, and to consciously build in a tolerance for experimentation and failure, and reward learning.

An important award we initiated in Nestle Nutrition was the "Borrow with Pride" award (where, famously, an idea from Bangladesh was scaled up and applied effectively in the US!!).

B) How can one develop "ambidextrous" leaders who can defend and re-imagine at the same time?

It is important to fit the leadership profile to the stage of the company on the "S curve" (see the following references). In the authors' experience, leaders can be broadly clustered into four distinct "competency buckets":

a. Entrepreneurial leaders who are creative and good at starting new businesses;

b. Leaders who are good at growing businesses;

c. Leaders who are good at cutting costs and closing businesses; and

d. Leaders who are good at deal making.

The first bucket calls for an "insurgent mindset". Risk-taking ability. Tolerance for failure and immense creativity and persistence. This profile can often be found by recruiting from people who have done startups (whether they failed or succeeded is not as important as what they learned).

The second bucket is where most leaders in growth organisations are to be found. People from the author's generation, who worked in large multinationals, learned to scale fast, deploy resources efficiently, lead across multiple cultures, and not "re-invent the wheel" any more than absolutely necessary.

The third bucket calls for competency in cutting costs, streamlining operations. Skills which are in great demand by PE companies.

The fourth bucket calls for "deal making" skills essential in successful M&A. This is a specialised skill set, often found in investment bankers.

Managers and leaders need to consciously develop an understanding of the different leadership profiles required by different parts of the business. An obvious question is "how can you develop ambidextrous leaders who can straddle two or more leadership requirements?".

- One good way to develop such leaders is to deliberately throw leaders, early in their careers, into roles they are not familiar with. The ones who show learning agility and the ability to develop ambidextrous capabilities are then put on a fast track.

- This also applies to cultural adaptability. Put people into unfamiliar cultures and then see how well they can adapt. This is an important function of transferring people into different geographies. A function that large companies would do well to bear in mind, even as they look to localise operations to reduce costs.

- A key question is "how does one get change agents and mavericks on board, and then manage, motivate, and inspire them to create?" and "how to insulate them from different stage cultures that do not value non conformity?". How to protect them from the stigma of "failure" that inevitably accompanies experiments?

  So, in fact, beyond recruitment, there has to be a support system to specifically nurture and protect ambidexterity, led by a sponsor from the executive board to protect, mentor, and nurture such managers. Especially from traditionally under-represented groups, like women, for instance.

- Simultaneously, companies would do well to get onto their supervisory (non-executive) boards people who have skills and exposure to one or more of these stage cultures. Most large company boards tend to lack people with venture capital or startup exposure, combined with "growth phase" exposure earlier on in their careers. They would do well to specifically look for such talent to bring on board.

4. IN SUMMARY

Above all, it is visionary and courageous leadership that will set the winners apart. Companies that merely wonder or speculate what change is coming their way will, in fact, be the future dinosaurs.

- Instead, visionary leadership creates, identifies, and then drives change to reinvent business models and make incumbents the new dinosaurs. Visionary leadership starts with defining, understanding, and asking about purpose.

  PURPOSE: WHY do we exist as an organisation.

  WHO do we add value to. And **HOW**.

  And what **VALUES** define the boundaries we will follow in this process.

Once this is done, share this widely within your teams, and repeatedly, in order to remind others "why we exist".

- Millennials (and innovators, likewise) are looking for companies with a purpose that resonates with them.

It is a critical leadership task to define, understand, and above all, protect this **PURPOSE** and **CORE VALUES** when responding with agility to disruptive change, whatever the source. Don't let expediency and short-cuts subvert your purpose.

Have a process in place to safeguard this and revisit it periodically. Otherwise, very quickly, you might find yourselves taking a road you did not intend to take.

And, thereafter, be very open-minded to change everything else.

Appendix
What disruption means for you: Specific lessons for insurgents

- If one is a startup, the focus is "value creation" and organisational culture is necessarily characterised by brainstorming, experimentation, and rapid prototyping. How one balances this with the focus on cash flow, customer delight, and discipline is a key initial challenge to work through consciously.

> The authors define here a **"Beanstalk"** to be a successful unidimensional startup which has scaled rapidly, but is focused on ONE product/service/customer. As a result, even while being successful, it's narrow and focused base makes it vulnerable.
>
> A beanstalk therefore needs to simultaneously do two things really well:
>
> - Scale rapidly the existing MVP
>
> - Re-invent wormholes into adjacencies that can broaden the base
>
> Each calls for distinct culture and people talents. Beanstalks need ambidextrous leaders as much as large incumbents do.

- If one is a "beanstalk", the cultural challenge is to reduce the amount of experimentation that one had when reinventing the MVP (the MVP works, which is why one is scaling up).

  And create a culture where the focus of experimentation and invention is "how to grow faster?". And "how to expand to adjacencies to make the trunk of the beanstalk more robust?".

- If the MVP is not gaining traction, what is the right time to close the business? Pull the plug? Sell the business?

We know that 90%+ of startups worldwide fail within the first two years. The reasons for failure are many, from an improperly conceived value proposition, inadequate funding, or weak execution.

Some companies however, survive and prosper.

I. WHICH STARTUPS MAKE IT BIG?

Based on the authors' experience as angel investors and venture capitalists, we can list eight characteristics:

i. Start with a real problem faced by customers (do NOT start with "tech" that appears to be "cool"), then pursue the resolution of this problem with evangelistic fervour. Invest time, money, resources. Ideate, be foolish, experiment rapidly initially, test, fail, and learn; get an MVP ready to figure out solutions to this problem. (Minimum viable proposition.)

ii. Ensure you can build some protection around this MVP. Are you the first mover in this problem definition? Do you have any intellectual property that can help build a competitive moat? Could you acquire data and refine your algorithms fast enough to build this moat?

iii. Make big bets on the future and the value proposition that will change the world. Startups like Pepperfry, Curefit, Office Ambience, or Mama Earth identified their target segment, problem identification, and core value proposition, then invested big to realise their potential fast.

There is a key difference between startups focussed on using technology to disrupt incumbents in the consumer goods market and those creating a completely new service that is digital in nature.

The former can use the advantages of tech (we discussed earlier) in building connections to highly focussed groups of consumers, using e-commerce and digital marketing (large incumbents find this not lucrative). But, while early wins can be fast, scaling up is not easy. Here is where we see the entry of aggregators (the Thracio model in the US or Mensa brands in India) which are able to scale incumbents rapidly.

A purely digital offering (on a fintech play, for instance) comes with greater risks of early failure, regulatory oversight, etc., but with greater chances of scaling up once the initial MVP is worked out.

iv. Attract talent. Early. And get them buying into the new religion. Mobilise people. Get a team together that buys into this with the same passion. Then continuously expand your religion. Be the key sales person. Be fanatical in your self-belief because you will find many detractors, many people who will tell you "why your idea will not work". Listen to them, address their concerns, if possible, but do not let your core belief be shaken.

However, as Costas Markides observes, there is a fine line that divides persistence (which is a virtue) and "being persistently foolish" by not looking at customer trends.

A key metric is: "Are customers willing to pay a price for your product or service?". Or at the very least, "Is you user base large enough to attract advertising revenue?".

v. If possible, get your customers to fund your growth by cash advances. (The authors recommend the book *The Customer-Funded Business*, by John

Mullins.) They will keep you focussed on customer value delivery and not allow any deviations.

A key metric that people look at in valuing startups is: "How many customers or users do you have on your platform, how satisfied are they, and how fast is this base growing?". The ability to scale fast is key.

Or are you losing early customers because they are dissatisfied?

vi. Focus on cash flow. A key reason many startups fail is because they do not understand this basic principle. Businesses run on cash.

Know how long of a cash runway you have ahead, given your current cash burn. Be very tight on spending. Resist the temptation to follow a funding round with indiscriminate hiring. Do not fall into the trap of going on a hiring binge without looking two years ahead. Speed is important but not at the cost of cash management.

Then work to extend this runway by improving your cash-conversion cycle within your operations . . . OR by raising more funds.

vii. The composition of the founding team should ensure a mix of complementary competencies. Missing any one sets one up for failure. The three key tasks are:

- Continuously being in "selling mode" by raising finance to extend the cash runway so that you have time to build the business. Many startups fail simply because they run out of cash.

- Have someone who runs the operations with tight control on key metrics. Customer satisfaction. Cost control. (This is key. Do NOT hire too far ahead of your cash forecasts.)

- Have someone who has the technical competencies (the CTO) who focuses on building the competitive moat through proprietary technology.

viii. Plan the transition from stage 1 (ideation, experimentation) to stage 2 (scaling up). As one scales up, refine and optimise the initial MVP, but do not keep reinventing it.

Startups are often started with missionary zeal by the founder. As they innovate, create, experiment, discover, eventually develop a successful MVP, and acquire scale, they face a key stumbling block to enter "stage 2".

How does the founder let go? How to hire people, trust them, incentivise, and measure performance? And how to trust key managers?

And how to let go of the "foolishness" that characterised their "discovery" phase? This is often a key stumbling block for startups because they are addicted to reinventing the value proposition. Continuously upgrading the MVP is necessary to improve the customer experience and to stay competitive while building competitive advantage. But not completely re-designing your offering every six months, so much that you confuse everybody.

Finally, know what is the right time to exit. And to whom. (Hopefully a "strategic" buyer.) So that one's "baby" is well-placed to succeed with (hopefully) better resources than one could bring to bear.

But also, one unlocks value as a founder and for fellow angel investors who bet on the startup in the first place. Keep assessing the demand for one's equity share. The market goes through ups and downs. And it is important to move beyond emotions to capture value at the right time.

2. WHAT ARE THE SPECIFIC TOOLS AND KNOWLEDGE RESOURCES AVAILABLE TO STARTUPS?

i) "Do you wish to be a Billionaire?" you are asked at Singularity University when you join. "Then start by identifying a problem faced by a billion people"! And then "re-imagine" a solution.

The basic idea is to focus on a problem faced by a large section of society. Or business. Look for the trade-offs along the value chain where middlemen charge a "rent".

Do not start with "technology" as the reason for your startup.

ii) Envision the change that you can create. Get this vision fixed in your mind, then start to evangelise and get people on board. Customers. Team members. Venture capitalists.

iii) Network with other founders and learn from their experiences and failures.

iv) In his book *From Zero to One*, Peter Thiel talks about the basic rules of a successful startup. This book would be a recommended bible for startups.

"Look for a problem worth solving", he says, "then apply tech to create a 10X improvement on legacy solutions".

Focus on a niche till you figure out your minimum value proposition (test/fail/repeat till you refine this) and then grow (because of your 10X value proposition) to dominate the niche.

v) Then, and only then, expand to adjacencies. Until then do not allow your-self to get distracted.

vi) Get a professional board and ensure governance processes are in place early.

Professional boards imposed by VCs can help force this change in mindset, often by hiring external CEO or COO. But at a cost, as discussed earlier.

VCs would do well to answer the question: "How to play to the founders' capabilities instead of forcibly asking them to play unfamiliar roles, especially as you scale?".

vii) Think of exit strategies for your early investors. Is it through a buy out? Who are the potential buyers and can you get them on board as a strategic investor? Is it via an eventual IPO? Then work towards realising these exit strategies.

A venture capitalist friend, Srikant Sastri, observed,

"Startups are built for speed. Large companies are built for scale."

This quote contains an essential learning, irrespective of what size your company might be: it is important to understand where you are situated and play to your strengths.

Startups are well suited to be insurgents, who try and fail till they hit upon a profitable product/service/niche where they create value.

Established companies cannot play this game. They are better suited to keep a look out for successful insurgents, then buy them and use their proven ability to scale.

The authors have mentored and consulted across several startups as well as established companies, to appreciate the truth of this statement.

We can apply this model to Google, Facebook, Uber, or Amazon to under-stand their phenomenal success.

References and further reading:

On S curves: https://hbr.org/1998/05/evolution-and-revolution-as-organizations-grow

Julian Birkenshaw on what companies can do: https://hbr.org/2022/01/how-incumbents-survive-and-thrive

Julian Birkenshaw and Costas Markides on disruption: www.london.edu/think/iie-digital-disruption-podcast-one

Epilogue

We hope you have enjoyed journeying with us through this book and reflecting on the various concepts and provocations we have tried to tease out. And, in each case, reflecting on the implications: the "so what" for enterprise.

We hope also that the toolkits and frameworks embedded in various chapters help you in your organisation or help you as an individual as you give shape to your professional journey.

This book is a snapshot of what we see at this point in time. It is by no means exhaustive. Indeed, the pace of change will inevitably mean some big changes underway may have possibly been missed out. This also implies that this book will need to constantly updated to be relevant and contemporary.

We invite you, our reader, to help shape the future evolution of this book going forward, by sharing your insights and reflections with us. We look forward, to finding an appropriate and creative solution to providing an open-source access to add such inputs.

It is an exciting time to be alive and use the changes underway to help shape the world.

Index

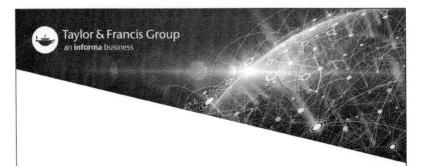